"Mi

She bru

wrong?

"I jus

Aggra ... head to avoid his searching look. After almost two weeks with barely a word, now he wanted to talk to her, and she was almost certain she knew what was on his mind.

"What about?"

Without waiting for permission, he settled himself beside her. Although he was watching her, Jenny kept her face averted.

After a moment, Benjamin reached out and pulled several strands of hay from her hair. Jenny could feel her heart start to pound as his breath fanned softly across her cheek. Somehow she didn't think that this little talk in such close proximity was a good idea.

"Jenny, look at me."

The moonlight shimmered around them, softly illuminating the area where they were sitting. His velvety voice sent a little flutter of excitement running through her. Reluctantly, she did as she was bid. Expecting censure, she found only sympathy in his dark mahogany eyes.

"Why don't you trust God?" he asked her gently.

DARLENE MINDRUP is a full-time homemaker and homeschool teacher. A "radical feminist" turned "radical Christian," Darlene lives in Arizona with her husband and two children. She believes "romance is for everyone, not just the young and beautiful."

Books by Darlene Mindrup

HEARTSONG PRESENTS
HP207—The Eagle and the Lamb
HP224—Edge of Destiny
HP243—The Rising Son
HP280—A Light Within
HP315—My Enemy, My Love

Drink from the Sky

Darlene Mindrup

Heartsong Presents

I would like to dedicate this book to my friend, Cindy Schooler. Thanks so much for the encouragement you give me. It's your turn now!

A note from the author:
I love to hear from my readers! You may correspond with me by writing:

Darlene Mindrup
Author Relations
PO Box 719
Uhrichsville, OH 44683

ISBN 1-57748-616-1

DRINK FROM THE SKY

Cover illustration by Victoria Lisi and Julius.

PRINTED IN THE U.S.A.

prologue

A young woman watched stealthily from behind a tree as the three men before her crowded around the paper they had just posted to the side of the general store. The larger of the three pushed back his stovepipe hat, sliding his hands into his pockets.

"That should bring some kind of response," he told the others, his southern drawl filled with satisfaction. They nodded their heads in agreement.

"Yep, even her own people should be more willing to turn her in for forty thousand dollars."

The dark-skinned girl recognized the speaker as the owner of the largest plantation in the area. His rotund belly heaved as he chuckled to himself. "What do you think, Carter?" He addressed himself to the man on his left, who had yet to speak. "Any wagers on how long it will be before she's brought to justice?"

The other man turned to his two companions, shrugging lightly. "No one has been able to catch her yet."

The larger man guffawed, throwing back his head with hearty laughter. "For forty thousand dollars most men would turn in their own mothers. That's not chicken feed, you know."

The man named Carter glanced slyly from one to the other. "Would you like to make a small wager, Greer?"

The other two glanced at each other before turning back to Mr. Carter. "What do you say, Compton? Wanna make a wager with old doubting Thomas here?"

Mr. Compton narrowed his eyes as he studied the man before him. "It would seem, suh, that your mother named you well. Yes, I'll make a small wager."

Thomas Carter grinned at both men. "Now understand, I

hope she'll be caught just as much as anybody, but I'm telling you the woman is half magician."

Compton blew out a short breath. "More like demon possessed," he told them. "Probably uses them heathen spells her family learned in Africa."

"Whatever it is," Carter agreed, "she'll really have to run for her money now." He chuckled at his unintended pun. "Buy you gentlemen a drink?"

Laughing, the trio headed for the nearest drinking establishment. The girl waited until they were well out of sight before dashing across the street to the position they had just vacated. Glancing quickly around, she read the sign posted to the building.

WANTED

Information to the whereabouts of the
slave, Harriet Tubman.
Reward
$40,000

The girl's mouth tilted up into a smile until her teeth gleamed against her ebony skin. So. Moses was at it again. She stifled a deep chuckle before her mahogany eyes darkened and the smile left her face.

Forty thousand dollars was a lot of money all right, but did those pompous windbags think for a minute that there was a darkie anywhere that would turn old Moses in? She spat on the sign, watching as her saliva slowly ran down the paper; then, turning, she just as slowly walked away.

one

"We can do it, Pappy. I knows we can."

The old man stared somberly at his daughter, his ebony skin glistening with sweat from the heat of the still, August evening. Even the crickets seemed to chirp lazily, drained by the warmth of this calm Tennessee night.

"What you wanna run away for, girl? Where you gonna go?"

Jenny reared back in surprise, blinking her dark mahogany eyes at her father. "What I wanna run away for? Don' you wanna be free? In the No'th we can have our *freedom*! You, mama, Jes, me."

Her father was already shaking his head. "I'se too old to go traipsing off somewheres I knows nothing about. How you gonna live, girl? *Where* you gonna live?"

"It don't matter," she told him, aggravated by his lack of enthusiasm. "We can find somethin'. Others do."

Old Jeb got up from the dilapidated rocker in front of the cold fireplace. He wandered slowly over to the doorway, and Jenny realized his rheumatism was acting up again. She glanced at the sky for signs of rain. Sure enough, through the window she could see dark clouds forming on the horizon. Jenny shivered. She hated storms ever since the time she had been a child working in the fields when she saw a bolt of lightning strike a mule. The young slave on the other end of the plow had been thrown at least twenty feet across the field. He had died later that night.

Jenny closed her eyes, but the picture refused to be dislodged. Even now, after twenty years, she couldn't forget the sight. She shivered again as she heard the rumble of thunder in the distance.

"My ole bones couldn't make such a trip," her father told her, staring pensively at the approaching storm. " 'Sides,

Massa Jackson ain't a bad man. He give us food, a place to live, clothes on our backs. Massa Jackson ain't never sold none of us what belongs to him. He a good man."

Jenny crossed to him, laying a hand against his forearm. She could feel the wrinkled skin beneath her fingers and realized that her father wasn't a young man anymore. She looked at him with new eyes. Maybe he was right. Maybe he couldn't make the trip. But wouldn't it be better to die trying for freedom than to stay here and rot as a slave?

When her father's glance caught hers, she realized he could tell every thought in her head. "Massa Jackson done said I could retire. He say I can live here all the rest of my days. How many men you know willing to do that?"

Feeling her skin heat, Jenny turned away. Pappy was right, Mr. Jackson was a good man. He fed and clothed his slaves, gave them Sundays off, made sure they had the doctor when they needed it. From other slaves she had talked to, Jenny knew this was an uncommon practice.

And Mr. Jackson was a devoted husband and father. *He* never looked at the female slaves the way some of the others did. Why even Amelia, Jenny's best friend, wore the brand of being half white.

Jenny almost sneered. Her own skin was as ebony as the coal that fired the pot-bellied stoves they cooked on at the big house. She was fiercely proud of the fact that both her parents were true Africans, Ashanti from the warrior tribe of the western part of Africa.

Sometimes Jenny felt the wildness of her kin stirring in her veins. Even now the thought of freedom made her blood run hot. She was surprised that her father, who had once been an Ashanti warrior, was so pacifistic in his acceptance of his captivity.

"Pappy," she cajoled. "Think what it would be like to live your life a free man!"

He sighed, his look filled with sadness. "I'se already free, girl. Jesus done set me free long time ago. I wish you could know Him, too, Jenny."

"Pappy," she told him in a determined voice, ignoring his religious nonsense, "I'm going as soon as I get a chance."

Before he could answer, the sky was lit by a huge bolt of light, immediately followed by a resounding clap of thunder. Neither one had noticed the storm's rapid approach or the darkness that filled the cabin.

Jenny squealed, diving for the bed in the corner. Her body shook violently as the wind beat against the cabin. Within moments, a torrent of rain began pounding on their tin roof.

❧

In the main house, Tilly stood at the door of the kitchen watching the driving rain. She fervently hoped Jes was not still in the fields. Wherever Jenny was, no doubt she had her head buried.

Tilly shook her head. Her daughter was so strong, so determined and self-sufficient, but she turned into a trembling child whenever a storm occurred. The mother understood, for many a night she had soothed her child after the horrible nightmares of that time so long ago.

A bell rang over the huge fireplace, and Tilly took off her apron, handing it to one of the serving girls. She went from the kitchen and made her way to the parlor, where Mrs. Jackson had been all morning in preparation for the return of her daughter.

"You wanted me, Missus Jackson?"

The woman turned china blue eyes upward, wrinkling her forehead in confusion. Even at the age of fifty-six, Sandra Jackson was a remarkably beautiful woman. She pushed back a curl of her elaborately coifed hair that even now held much of its original color.

"Tilly, what do you think? Should I invite the Jeffersons for the engagement party?"

Tilly smiled. It wasn't unusual for the woman of the house to ask advice of her slaves, for she didn't see them as such. Tilly had been present at the birth of Adelaide, the Jacksons' only child. After Tilly helped to resuscitate the infant, Mrs. Jackson had held Tilly in high esteem. They were more like friends than mistress and servant.

"Now, missus. You know Abe Jefferson done just about broke his heart over Miss Adelaide's engagement. He been in love with her fo' a long time now."

The frown increased. "I know, but his mama and papa have always been close friends of ours. I can't just not invite them, can I?"

Placing her hands on her hips, Tilly studied her mistress. "Iffen you invited 'em, they'd come, but I don' think Mr. Abe will. I betcha he'll find a reason not to."

The frown cleared. "Of course. How silly of me." She smiled at Tilly, rising to her feet. Her gown billowed round her as her hoops swayed from side to side. "Tell Eli to fetch the carriage, will you? He can hand deliver all the announcements."

Tilly followed her mistress from the room, shaking her head slightly. No wonder Mr. Jackson adored her. It was really hard not to.

❧

The storm passed and with it Jenny's fear. She rose from the bed and went to the door. One thing about such storms, they cleaned the air and scattered the mosquitoes. Jenny knew it wouldn't last long, though, so she was reluctant to open the door again.

Before long the room was like a bake oven, and Jenny knew she had no choice. Opening the door, she took a deep breath of the freshly washed air.

Her father was dozing in the rocking chair. Lips twisting up at the corners, Jenny studied the sleeping man; she grinned openly when he shook himself awake with a loud snore. He continued as though their conversation had never been interrupted.

"You gonna run away? And what if a storm comes, what you gonna do then? You think it ain't gonna rain anytime while you out on the road? Then you betta plan on leavin' in the winter, huh? But then you just might freeze ta death."

Jenny quailed at the thought of being caught out in a storm. It was almost enough to make her rethink her position. Almost.

She went to the kitchen area to begin preparing supper. Mama would be home soon, and she would be tired. Pulling a pan from the cupboard, Jenny dropped in a lump of lard. After lighting the fire in the fireplace, she placed the pan in the fireplace oven to melt the grease, while she began putting together the ingredients for cornbread.

Beating the batter gave her some satisfaction, and she continued doing so longer than she really needed to. Could she really leave Mama and Pappy? Her heart sank at the thought. They had to come with her. They just had to.

Pulling the pan from the oven beside the fireplace, Jenny wished again for the coolness of autumn. Having to use the fireplace to cook made eating an almost unenjoyable chore. She poured the batter into the melted grease and returned the pan to the oven.

Jenny knew that Pappy would talk with Mama about what she had told him. Would Mama see things her way, or would she side with her father?

She hadn't long to find out. A sound at the door indicated her mother's return. Sometimes Mama seemed to have second sight, and tonight was no exception. She glanced from one to the other.

"All right. What's goin' on here?"

Jenny's eyes refused to meet those of her mother. "Nothin'. Sit down, Mama. Supper's almost ready." When Jenny did manage to look at Mama, she met a determined look that Jenny knew she had no hope of thwarting. "Can we eat first?" she pleaded.

Her father rose to his feet. "I think tha's a good idea."

Tilly waited until they were seated around the table and grace had been said before fixing her daughter with an eloquent look. She said nothing, waiting for Jenny to speak.

Jenny's chin set in a determined line that more than matched her mother's. "I tole Pappy that I think we could run away to the No'th. They's enough folks on the Railroad to help us." Her eyes met her mother's, and at her surprised look, Jenny rushed on. "We could find a place up No'th and be free. We could have a good life."

"We have a good life here," Mama told Jenny flatly.

Angrily, Jenny rose to her feet. "But we not *free*!"

"What you talkin' about, girl? The Jacksons is good to us. Why, they almost like family. You and Miss Adelaide was raised together, like sisters. If it hadn't been fo' Miss Adelaide, you wouldn't even be able to write and read. She helped you learn, even though it was agin the law."

Jenny began to pace the floor in agitation. "I know all that. But I'm still not *free*! I wanna be free." Her voice lowered in pleading as she tried to make her parents see.

Tilly shook her head slowly. "What you gonna do in the No'th that you cain't do here?"

"I can marry who I want! I don' have to worry about my chillun being taken away from me. I don' have to worry about my husband being sold to someone else so he can be a stud for mo' little slaves."

"Mr. Jackson ain't never done no such thing, and he wouldn't, either," her father admonished gently. "He a good man."

"You keep saying that! But the point is, he *could* if he wanted to."

Her mother got up and began to clear the table. "The world could end tomorrow. I could die tomorrow. Jes's baby could be born tomorrow. Your pappy could go blind tomorrow. They's a bunch of things that *could* happen, but why worry 'bout 'em till they do?"

Jenny sighed in frustration. This was getting her nowhere. Her parents had obviously decided, and that was that. She knew from past experience that you could move a mountain easier than her parents when they had fixed something in their heads.

"I'm gonna go see Jes," she told them. Her parents watched her leave without saying a word.

She headed for her brother's cabin just a short distance away. Mr. Jackson had allowed Jes and Dinah to marry several months ago, and now they were expecting their first child. Would that child ever know freedom? Would Jes and Dinah want to come with her when she left?

Obviously not. Her brother faced her across the little cabin, his eyes shooting sparks of anger. "Are you outta yo' min'? What you mean comin' here and talking to us 'bout runnin' away? Girl, you gotta be crazy!"

"Don' you want yo' son to be free? Don' you wanna be?"

Jenny saw the fearful look Dinah gave her husband. Jes was a powerfully built man, his muscles evidence of the long hours he spent in the fields. Surely he wasn't afraid.

"Jenny," he told her, "if you runs away, they gonna come askin' us 'bout you. What you think we gonna tell 'em? Did you even stop to figger what this might mean to the rest of us? What they gonna do to *us*?"

"Come with me and they won' do nothin'."

Jes shook his head. "We don' wanna leave, Jenny. Massa Jackson, he good to us." He pulled his wife to his side. "What you think gonna happen to the baby if we try runnin' away?" He shook his head again. "No, Jenny. We gonna stay."

Jenny left their house feeling defeated. How could anyone in their right minds want to remain a slave if there was even the slightest chance of freedom? Her parents were old. In a way she could understand them. But Jes? He was young, strong. He had a family to think about. Here they would never be more than slaves at the whim of their master.

True, Master Jackson was a good man, but what if he changed? Jenny had seen such before.

When she returned to her cabin, her parents were already in bed. Tired out from their day's work, they were already asleep.

Dropping her dress to the floor, Jenny pulled her cotton nightdress over her head. She would have preferred sleeping without it in the almost unbearable heat, but her parents' conventional upbringing made her decide otherwise. She crawled into her pallet on the floor and stared up at the shadows created on the ceiling by the full moon peeking through the windows. Her thoughts raced around inside her head, one followed by another.

She wanted her freedom so badly she could almost taste it, but could she leave her family? What was she going to do now? If she stayed, she would be constantly chafing at her forced servitude, but if she left, she knew she would miss Mama and Pappy.

How long she lay there she didn't know, but a scratching at the shanty window brought her to her feet. Apparently her parents had not heard the sound, and Jenny hesitated, wondering if it had been her imagination.

When the scratching came again, it was followed by a soft whistle. Recognizing the sound, Jenny hurried to the door, unmindful of her night clothes. She closed the door behind her, listening carefully.

"Jenny, over here." The furtive whisper sent Jenny spinning around. Amelia crouched by the side of the shanty. She rose quickly to her feet, motioning Jenny to her side.

They walked a ways from the house and Jenny could feel her friend trembling at her side.

"Melia, what's the mattah with you? What you doin' here this time of night?"

Turning, Amelia clutched Jenny's arm. Her eyes gleamed in the semi-darkness. "Jenny, did you mean what you said 'bout runnin' away?"

Surprised, Jenny stopped walking. "What? What you talkin' 'bout?"

"You said you was gonna leave this here place. Remember? Well, I wanna come wit you."

"When?"

"I gotta leave befo' Friday. I heard the missus talkin' and she gonna send me south."

Jenny could feel the blood drain from her face. Going south meant never being seen or heard from again.

"Why she wanna do that?"

Amelia grimaced in the dark. "Why you think? She tired of lookin' at me and knowin' what her husband did. Maybe she think if she get rid of me, then she get rid of her shame. I don' know, I jus' know I *cain't* go south. I'd rather die."

Thinking quickly, Jenny told her friend, "Go back to the plantation. I got some thinkin' to do. Some plans to make. I won' let 'em send you south."

"What'll you do?"

"Miss Adelaide won' be comin' home till next week, so I won' be missed till then. Tomorrow's Thursday. I'll come fo' you tomorrow night. Be ready. When you hear me singin' 'bout the drinkin' gourd, you meet me at the edge of the woods borderin' Massa Greer's plantation. We gonna follow the drinkin' gourd to the No'th."

Both girls looked up at the night sky riddled with dots of light. Their eyes turned to the faint North Star and followed it downward to the drinking gourd, or what some called the Big Dipper.

"What you think that gourd's fo', Jenny? Why you think it placed in the sky that way?"

Jenny's voice came back, soft and gentle. "It's fo' people who want to drink of freedom. They just drink from the sky."

Amelia clutched Jenny's arm. "You won' change yo' min', will you?"

Jenny shook her head, her eyes still fixed on the North Star. "No. You go on home, now. I'll come fo' you tomorrow. If Moses can do it, so kin I."

Amelia snorted softly. "Moses, she had God on her side. So did the Moses of ole. *You* don' even believe in Him."

Jenny closed her lips tightly together. "Go on home, Melia. I come fo' you tomorrow."

After Amelia left, Jenny reluctantly returned to the cabin. She opened the door, trying to keep it from squeaking. Closing it softly behind her, she nearly jumped from her skin when her mother spoke from the darkness.

"What you been up to, girl?"

Thankful for the cover of darkness to hide her giveaway face, Jenny told her mother, "Nothin', Mama. I jes couldn't sleep. It's way too hot."

Jenny could sense through the darkness her mother's disbelief, but Mama didn't say anything. Jenny lay back down in her bed, for the first time realizing what she had just done. She had committed herself to an act that could have serious repercussions for her family.

In that moment of decision, her thoughts clarified. It would be best if her family knew nothing of her plans, because then when they were questioned, as they most assuredly would be, they could with honesty say they knew nothing.

A flash of lightning in the distance made her heart suddenly start to pound. It was one thing to talk brave, but quite another to pull it off. What on earth had her impulsiveness caused her to do now?

two

Jenny watched impatiently as the sun sank slowly below the horizon. The crickets began their nightly chorus, and Jenny could hear the sound of the field slaves singing in the distance.

She smiled as she recognized the song they used to make fun of the master. The words seemed harmless enough, but anyone who knew Mr. Greer would recognize him in the lyrics. Only Mr. Greer, as mean as he was, could inspire such humor in the plantation slaves. It was either laugh or do something utterly drastic. They chose the former.

Jenny could see the lanterns and torches bobbing along the fields. Although Mr. Jackson allowed his slaves to end their day at sundown, Mr. Greer's overseer forced his slaves to work sometimes until midnight.

The workers were making their way toward the huge storage barns where their tobacco pickings for the day would be weighed. Jenny knew that if Mr. Greer's workers came up short, they would feel the whip. As far as she knew, there had never been a day yet that everyone reached their quota. She hoped and prayed that Amelia would.

Before long Jenny heard the sound of the whip being eagerly wielded and the screams that followed. Covering her ears with her hands, she tried to block out the horrible sound. A sob tore at her throat as the repercussions of her own foolish action permeated her mind.

If she were caught, would the same thing be done to her? Would her parents suffer the same fate? For the first time in a very long while, she offered up a prayer for their protection.

Finally, the sounds from the plantation grew quiet, and slowly Jenny pulled her hands from her ears. She was shivering, and she knew it was only partly from the dropping temperatures.

What seemed an eternity later, Jenny heard the call of a whippoorwill close by. Recognizing the sound, she puckered her lips and returned the call. Almost instantly, she heard the soft shuffle of hurrying feet.

A moment later Amelia came into view. Quickly she made her way to Jenny's side, dropping to the ground beside her. Her breathing was labored, and Jenny frowned as she searched her friend's features for some sign of trouble. Amelia's face was pale, a mere reflection of the quarter moon rising in the sky above them.

"Melia? What's wrong?"

For a moment Amelia didn't answer. Finally, she lifted her head, staring solemnly at Jenny. "I didn't make my quota today."

Sucking in a sharp breath, Jenny tried to turn the girl around. She shrugged out of Jenny's hold, but there were tears in her eyes.

"No. I didn't git beat. Nathan. . .Nathan saw I didn't have enough, so he. . .he give me some of his. I tried to give it back, but he wouldn't take it." A sob shook her. "So they beat him 'stead of me."

Jenny felt her heart drop. Nathan and Amelia had been sweethearts for some time, but Mr. Greer didn't know about it. Neither did Mr. Hawkins, the overseer, or there would surely be trouble. Mr. Hawkins had had his eye on Amelia for some time. Both Amelia and Nathan knew it was only a matter of time before old Hawk would claim Amelia, and there would be nothing they could do about it. Even if Mr. Greer were to allow Nathan and Amelia to marry, that wouldn't stop Hawk from claiming Amelia in the long, dark nights.

The thought of Nathan lying on the ground beside the gin house bleeding caused Jenny to hesitate. He could bleed to death, if he wasn't dead already. She could see from her expression that the same thoughts were flitting through Amelia's mind.

Jenny sighed. "We cain't help Nate now. The others will care for him."

Amelia nodded. "I knows that, but it still hard to leave him."

Rising to her feet, Jenny glanced around the woods. "We gotta git 'fore the paddy rollers come."

Eyes going wide with fear, Amelia rose slowly to stand beside her friend. "You gots a plan, Jenny? Where we goin'?"

Jenny raised a clenched fist to her mouth, biting on her knuckle. "I gots food for the journey, but all I knows to do is to follow the North Star."

"That's it? That's all the plan you gots?"

Glaring at the other girl, Jenny asked her, "You gots a better one?"

They stood facing each other a long moment before Amelia finally dropped her eyes to her feet. Shaking her head, she hunched her shoulders forward in an attitude of defeat.

Jenny grew angry. "Stan' up straight, you hear me? As of this moment, you ain't no slave no mo'. You understand me?"

There was no smile to follow the words, and Jenny hoped her friend realized she was in dead earnest. Lifting her chin, Amelia straightened her shoulders. "I hears."

Jenny lifted the pack of food from the ground. "Good."

A sudden noise caught their attention. Jenny could hear her own heart thundering in her ears. Amelia clung to Jenny as though she would offer some protection, but they both knew there was nothing either of them could do if they were caught. Paddy rollers, those men hired by the whites to search the woods at night for slaves, were notorious for the savage beatings they delivered. Their usual job was to break up any religious meetings the slaves might be having, but they were always on the lookout for runaways.

"Shhh." Jenny pushed Amelia behind a large pine tree and moved away from her. The rustling was growing closer. Lifting a tree limb from the ground, Jenny prepared to use it if necessary. She glanced across at Amelia. "If I tell you to run, do it!"

Planting her feet squarely on the path, Jenny lifted the limb with both hands. Suddenly, a figure broke from the cover of the trees, and Jenny recognized him just a moment before she would have clobbered him with her club.

She dropped the limb and hurried across to the staggering figure. "Nate! Nate, what you doin' here?"

Nate dropped against Jenny, his eyes rolling back into his head. "I'se comin', too, Jenny. I cain't let you and Melia wander 'round this country widout some protection." His panting voice ceased, and Jenny felt the whole of his body weight as it sagged against her.

Gently she helped him to the ground as Amelia rushed to their side. Dropping to her knees, Amelia took the big man's head onto her lap. "Oh, Nate, Nate," she sobbed, rocking him back and forth. "What I done to you? Dear Lord, don' let my Nathan die."

Nate wore no shirt, and Jenny could see the blood congealing against the welts that ran across his back and over his shoulders. Sucking in a breath, she knelt beside him, pulling some salt from her pack. Amelia's eyes widened. "Jenny! Where'd you git that salt? Girl, if they catch you stealing. . ." Her voice trailed off as her worried eyes fixed on Jenny's face.

Amused, Jenny answered her friend without lifting her eyes from the injured man. "If they catch me, they ain't gonna be worried 'bout no salt. 'Sides, I don' care. I thought we might need it."

At the time, Jenny had been unsure why she had taken the salt. Some inner voice seemed to compel her, much as she wished to disregard it. Now she was thankful that she had listened.

Hurriedly, Jenny and Amelia turned Nate gently and applied salt to the open wounds. Nate groaned, trying to lift himself from the ground.

"Boy, you ain't goin' nowheres," Jenny told him stoutly. "Ain't no way you can make it far as we gots to go."

Jenny was surprised when he managed to stand, a look of resolution settling over his features. He took a deep, steadying breath. "I'se goin', Jenny, an' you cain't stop me."

They glared at one another a full minute before Jenny

shrugged her shoulders. "Fine! Gets us all kilt."

He shook his head, flinching as he reached down to lift Jenny's pack. "I ain't gonna git nobody kilt. I be fine in a few minutes. Let's go."

"Gimme that!" Jenny told him as she jerked the pack from his nerveless fingers. "You jes hang onto Melia, you hear me?"

Nate's teeth gleamed against his dark skin. "Yes, ma'am."

Jenny took the lead, her eyes continually watching the sky and her northern compass. The drinking gourd was bright tonight, perhaps in celebration of their quest for freedom. For a moment Jenny felt almost invincible, like nothing could stop her now.

How long they traveled, Jenny was unsure, but suddenly they could hear the sounds of baying dogs in the distance. Amelia clung to Nate, her face twisted with fear.

"How could they know so soon?" Jenny whispered, paralyzed by terror.

Nate looked grim. "Hawk musta. . ." He stopped, pulling Amelia close. "I'd like to kill that man!"

Amelia touched his face softly. "No, Nate. That's not what Jesus would do. We gots to fo'give people what hurts us."

His angry eyes blazed down into hers. "You gonna fo'give him when he takes you? You gonna fo'give him then?"

Jenny interrupted. "He ain't gonna take Melia. Nor you, either."

"How we gonna git away? Them's bloodhounds they usin'."

Jenny's eyes suddenly gleamed. "We gots to split up."

"What?" Both Amelia and Nate were looking at her as though she had lost her mind.

"Nate, you take Melia and head east. They gonna,'spect us to head no'th. I'll stay here till you gits fur enough away, then I gonna erase you tracks. I'll git the dogs to follow me no'th."

"No!" Amelia and Nate were both shaking their heads. "We stay together."

"You do what I tells you, you hear?" Jenny glared at each one in turn. "Mr. Jackson, he won't beat me if I gits caught.

Pappy right about him bein' a good man. But don't make no never mind no how, cause I ain't gonna git caught. Pappy taught me a few tricks 'bout huntin'." She smiled at them, the light of determination shining in her eyes. "Now git! They gittin' closer."

Reluctantly, Nate pulled Amelia forward. Jenny could see that the adrenaline was pumping through his veins; fear had given him an extra spurt of strength. "God be wit you, Jenny."

Turning, they hurried off, and soon they were hidden by the darkness and the surrounding trees.

Jenny could hear the dogs getting closer, but she could move faster now without the other two. Taking a branch with forked limbs that was lying beside her, Jenny began brushing the leaves of the forest like a broom. She went quite a distance toward where the other two had recently been traveling, and then started pulling the underbrush backward toward her.

Finally, she stomped all over the gathered leaves and brush. For extra measure, she took a piece of fat pork from her sack; after rubbing it on the bottom of her feet, she headed north. She moved quickly, but the dogs were gaining on her. Suddenly, their baying ceased, and Jenny knew they had reached the area where she and the others had parted.

She stopped, listening to see if her ruse had worked. Abruptly, the baying resumed, and Jenny could hear the animals moving in her direction. Smiling slightly, she started to run. She knew a stream was close by, and if she could only reach it, she could further confuse the dogs. It wouldn't be for long, but perhaps long enough.

When she broke into the open, she could hear the water just ahead of her. Before long, she came to the banks of what should have been a small creek but, due to the recent rains, was instead a raging torrent. She hesitated, knowing she couldn't swim, but the swollen stream couldn't be much past her knees, though from its rushing intensity, it seemed much larger.

Jenny realized that if not for the rain, the creek would have been too small to hinder the bloodhounds in their pursuit of her. Now, with the stream swollen to twice its size, it would work perfectly. Mama would have called it Divine Providence, and for a moment Jenny felt guilty for her rejection of her mother's God.

Aggravated with herself, she pushed herself forward until she felt the water around her ankles, then up to her knees. The water was refreshing to her bare feet. They ached horribly, and for a moment she regretted giving Amelia her shoes, but only for a moment.

Mr. Greer gave as little to his slaves as possible. Most of the women either had a shift or a dress, but not both, and very few of the men had shirts, only their pants. She wondered how Nate would fare. If anyone saw the stripes on his back, they would know he was a runaway. If she had had an extra shirt, she would have gladly given it to him, but she didn't. Jenny just hoped that the God Amelia believed in so strongly would take care of them. Frankly, she had her doubts. What had God ever done for her, anyway? She had been a slave all her life, and if that was a reason to worship God, she'd just as soon forego the pleasure.

She could hear the hounds getting closer now. There was no way she could outrun them, even if the water did throw them off her scent. She had to find a refuge and hope that she could hide.

As she waded upstream, her eyes caught sight of a branch from a huge willow tree dragging its feathery fingers in the water. She quickly made her way to it and, taking a firm hold, pulled herself out of the water and up onto the branch. Before long, she had shinnied her way almost to the tree's top, clinging to its rough surface as her heart began to thunder in time to the rushing stream.

Would the dogs find her here, or had she walked far enough upstream to confuse them? She would know in a moment, because their baying was drawing ever closer.

The dogs burst from the trees and from her vantage point at the top of the tree she could see them in the distance. They circled the area where she had entered the stream, their barks turning to confused whimpers.

Several men broke into the clearing behind them, and Jenny recognized Mr. Hawkins, his rifle pointing toward the ground.

She couldn't hear what they were saying, but the tone of voice carried clearly on the balmy night air. It was obvious they were having some kind of argument. The man with the dogs slipped on their leads and began walking the dogs upstream along the bank.

Hawk hesitated only a moment before he turned to the other men and sent them in the opposite direction. Then turning back, he followed the man with the dogs. Jenny knew he would try to find where she had come out of the water. Hopefully the way she had climbed the tree on the outermost limb would leave no scent for the dogs to pursue, but she knew that bloodhounds had a sharp sense of smell.

When the men stopped under her tree, Jenny thought her heart would stop also. Hardly daring to breathe, she listened to their conversation.

"I tell you, they're gonna go downstream!" That was Hawk's voice.

"Look, Hawkins. You wanna do this searchin' by yourself, or you wanna let me do my job?"

"Give me them dogs," Hawk growled, "and I could do it a sight better than you."

"What makes you think they gonna go downstream anyway?"

" 'Cause there are folks down that way that are part of the Underground Railroad. That's where they'll head."

There was silence for a full minute. "If you know that, how come you ain't told the law?"

"I ain't got no proof."

"Then how do you know?"

Hawk was growing impatient now. "I just do. Now we gonna head that way, or you gonna traipse up and down this creek bank all night?"

The other man's bark was almost as fierce as his dogs.

"Have it your way. Ain't no skin off my nose." The dogs yelped as he jerked them around. As they turned to leave, Jenny switched position slightly to better see their departure. As she did, a small branch cracked and hurtled downward toward the water.

"What was that?" Hawk hissed.

"I don't know. Came from this tree, I think."

Jenny's heart seemed to stop altogether. Her teeth ached from clenching her jaw. She could hear the men circling the tree. If she could just sit still, they couldn't see her, even with the light from the moon.

She could hear movement below, but she couldn't tell what was happening. She almost fell from her perch when she heard Hawk yelp.

"Look out! It's a moccasin!"

Instead of striking terror into her as it normally would have, the sudden boom of the gun reassured Jenny. She had forgotten that water moccasins love willow trees. It was a miracle she hadn't encountered the snake herself.

She felt the blood drain from her face. Surely she should have met up with the beast sooner or later, but again she had been spared. Conflicting feelings of rebellion and a desire to embrace the protection of the Almighty waged a war inside of her.

The men began moving away, their receding voices drifting back to her.

"Did it git you?"

She could see Hawk as he moved across the clearing below the tree. He spat on the ground, his tobacco juice leaving a dark spot in the dirt.

"Naw, and he ain't gonna git no one else, neither. Not anymore."

Both men chuckled and that was the last sound Jenny heard as they disappeared from her view.

She continued sitting in the tree for some time, trying to decide just how long she should do so. What if when the dogs couldn't find her trail downstream they came back? Still, night was the only time she was free to move. She would have to hide during the day. But where?

The wind whistled through the branches, moving the limbs gently. Or was it the wind? Could there be another moccasin up here, slithering its way toward her? Jenny felt her skin crawl, she shivered and shimmied back down the tree, careful to watch where she placed her hands.

As she dropped herself back into the creek, Jenny flinched at the small splash she made. She stopped, listening intently. No sounds came to her except the night's quiet sounds. Jenny had never been afraid of the woods. She loved the sounds of tree frogs, crickets, and owls. That's how she and Amelia had been able to be such close friends, for Amelia loved the woods, too. Often they met between the two plantations late at night when they should have been sleeping. There was something so. . .so *free* about being among the trees shrouded in darkness. Their dark skin camouflaged them as effectively as the little salamanders that wandered through the area.

Jenny stood in the middle of the creek trying to decide which way to go. It made sense to head in the opposite direction from the men, but Hawk had mentioned someone from the Underground. Could she find them? And if she did, would they be willing to help her?

More than likely, Hawk would catch her, but then again Hawk didn't really know her. He wouldn't realize that she had helped Amelia escape. At least she *hoped* she had helped Amelia to escape.

Deciding that she would rather help herself than risk facing Hawk again, Jenny turned and headed farther upstream. Her eyes swiftly scanned the sky, searching for the drinking gourd. Finding it, she breathed a sigh of relief. As long as the star was there to point the way, she would be just fine.

The water was cold against her feet as she treaded her way slowly upstream. She should leave the water soon, but she was reluctant to do so. The longer she stayed in the water, the better her chances of fooling the dogs.

Her teeth began to chatter as the night wore on. How far had she come anyway? Four miles? Five? If she continued in this direction, she would eventually reach the source of this creek. Already the water was beginning to thin.

When she started to sneeze, she decided it was time to leave the water. Not knowing how far she had come, she pressed forward on the bank. Her feet were bruised and aching from the rocks in the stream, but she doggedly placed one foot in front of the other.

The eastern sun was just peeking over the horizon when she decided to stop and rest. She sat and watched the glorious sunrise, its red and orange rays bursting upon the earth in ever-changing patterns of light. How did that saying go? Red sky at night, sailor's delight. Red sky in the morning, sailors take warning? Jenny felt her heart sink. Please. Not a storm.

She knew who she was asking, but she wouldn't admit it to herself. Religion was a tool used by whites to keep blacks as slaves. No. She wanted no part of the white man's religion. She could still hear the white preacher hired for the slaves quoting from the Bible about slaves obeying their masters and how this would please God. If the shoe were on the other foot, she doubted they would feel the same.

As the sun rose higher, Jenny sought for some kind of shelter. She finally found a small cave among the rocks and wedged herself into it. The ground was damp, and the rocks dripped with moisture. Shivering again, she tried to make herself comfortable enough to sleep. Exhaustion from lack of sleep and nervous tension finally took its toll and she drifted into a deep slumber.

The sun was descending from its zenith when she finally awakened. Her stomach rumbling told her what had roused her. Pulling her pack to her chest, she dug among its contents for something to eat. Pulling out an apple, Jenny rubbed it on her sleeve before taking a big bite. The juice rolled down her chin, and she sucked it back into her mouth. She had plenty of apples, because Mrs. Jackson always left some on the trees for the slaves to enjoy. Well, enjoy them she would.

She felt a pang as she realized Mama and Pappy would be sick with worry about her. They would know she had left by now. Her pang turned into a full-scale worry when she thought about how her absence would affect them. Had they been questioned? Would anyone believe them when they told them they knew nothing? Tears came to her eyes as she considered the pain she was causing her parents. She only hoped that emotional pain was *all* they would suffer.

After the sun sank below the horizon, Jenny crawled from her hole, stretching her cramped muscles. She took a step, and then sucked in a breath at the pain that wrenched its way through her feet. She sat down and began to massage her aching feet. She simply *had* to do something about getting some shoes, but just what she could do, she had no idea. Well, for now, she would just have to suffer.

Forcing herself to her feet, she began to slowly make her way down the little crest of rocks. When she looked at the sky, her heart sank. Clouds moved swiftly across the moon, hiding the drinking gourd from sight. Now how was she supposed to find her way? If she just started traveling, she might just find herself heading south. And then what? She shuddered at the possibilities.

Those clouds told her that it was going to rain, and she could only hope that that would be all it would do. She decided to follow the stream northward and hope that it headed directly north. Sometimes streams twisted and turned, and goodness only knew where she might wind up.

When morning came, Jenny again took refuge, thankful that she had come this far. She was growing weary, but she chastised herself for her failing courage, knowing that she still had a long way to go. Her throat was sore, her muscles ached, and she wanted nothing more than to put her head in Mama's lap and feel her soothing touch on her hot forehead. She knew she was running a fever, but she didn't stop to worry about it. Now was not the time to give in to sickness.

For two more days she traveled northward, sometimes in a driving rain, and this, combined with the dropping temperatures at night, only served to increase her illness. She should be about halfway to Kentucky by now, she reasoned, but she really had no way of knowing. It mattered little to her, because Kentucky was a slave state, too. Her goal was to cross the Ohio River into Indiana. Only then would she be considered free, and then only as long as she wasn't captured and returned.

Ever since the Fugitive Slave Act had been passed in 1850, many slaves had been caught in free states and returned to their owners. Jenny was determined that wouldn't happen to her. She was headed for Canada and nothing was going to stop her. She would make it or die trying.

When she settled herself the next day for some much needed rest, every muscle in her body was aching, and her throat was raw from coughing. She was utterly miserable and longed for the comfort only her mother could offer.

She had to literally crawl out of her shelter that evening, for her legs refused to hold her. Burying her head in her arms, she lay prostrate upon the ground, letting the tears come. She couldn't go on, she just couldn't. She had no more energy left.

How long she lay there was impossible to tell. Each minute, each hour, seemed to roll into one. Jenny felt herself losing awareness. Trying to focus her mind was an impossibility.

She felt herself lifted from the ground into strong, warm arms, and she felt a security she had never felt before as she was cuddled against a powerful chest. Jenny could feel a mighty heartbeat as they began to move, and a soft, deep voice came soothingly into her consciousness.

The words were unclear to her cloudy mind, but the safety they conveyed was not. Only one person she knew could possibly make her feel this way and, smiling, she murmured His name.

"Jesus."

three

“How is she, Benjamin?”

Benjamin Walters lifted himself from the side of the bed where he had been perched. His height took him well above the woman standing beside him. Her pert gray eyes were lifted inquiringly to his face.

Edda Freeman was a mighty fine woman. A saint of God if ever there was one. Benjamin gave her one of his rare smiles, and her wrinkled face creased into a return smile, her gray hair a perfect match for her gentle eyes.

“She’s as well as can be expected under the circumstances,” Benjamin told her, rubbing a large hand across his kinky hair. “She’s alive, but that’s about all I can say of her right now.” He began putting away his instruments into his black bag. Snapping it shut, he straightened, the smile gone from his face. “She has pneumonia.”

“I was afraid of that.” Edda pulled the covers up higher against the girl’s chest.

Benjamin stared down at the girl, his brown eyes dark with pity. He noticed that her skin was a shade darker than his own mahogany brown as he lifted her wrist from the covers to check her pulse. “She’s obviously a runaway. I wonder where she’s from.”

Jacob Freeman came to stand beside them, tucking a hand beneath his wife’s arm. “Don’t know. Haven’t heard of anyone looking for a runaway.” His eyes studied the still figure on the bed. “What will thee do, Benjamin?”

Sighing, Benjamin turned and made his way across the small room to the kitchen beyond. He pulled out a chair and seated himself at the table, reaching for his now lukewarm coffee. “I don’t know, Jacob.” Forehead puckering into a frown,

Benjamin began drumming his fingers against the red and white checkered tablecloth. "I don't feel right just leaving her."

"How did thee happen to find her, Benjamin?" Edda inquired as she joined him at the table. "We didn't expect thee again for some time."

Benjamin concentrated on his cup, twisting it around and around. He knew he would have to tell them, but he was reluctant. These gentle people were fierce in their determination not to wreak physical violence on anyone, even though they were as fiercely committed to helping runaways. Benjamin, on the other hand, was not reluctant at all and he would do whatever needed doing to free his people from the bonds of slavery.

"I heard about a slave coffle heading this way from northern Kentucky. Mainly recaptured slaves from farther south being taken back, but there are others as well."

Jacob was surprised. "Isn't that unusual for this time of year? The cotton picking just started. I wouldn't think anyone would part with their slaves right now."

"Normally, you would be right," Benjamin agreed. "But since Mr. Lincoln's election, many whites have panicked, believing that he will set all the slaves free. They intend to make a profit before that can happen, so there is a rush to sell slaves to those who believe it will never happen."

"It's a pity," Edda sighed. Her eyes focused unflinchingly on Benjamin's face. "But what do thee intend to do?"

Benjamin met her eyes, his own never wavering. "Whatever I have to. Fortunately, most slave drivers consider blacks to be as stupid as animals, so when I confront them, they are so surprised that I rarely have to use violence."

"And what of the girl?"

Benjamin's eyes went beyond the couple sitting across from him to the still figure on the bed. He shook his head. "She will need time to recover. I have already told you all that needs to be done for her and left you medicine that should help, but only time will tell. There is nothing more that I can do for her right now. If I wait, I might miss the slave coffle." He sighed heavily. "I'll just have to plan a return trip in the near future."

"I will leave supplies in the millhouse, as per usual," Jacob told him.

"Thanks, Jacob. Have I ever told you two just how much I appreciate you?"

Edda's eyes twinkled back at him. "A time or two."

Benjamin's even white teeth gleamed as his lips curved upward. "Well, I hope you don't get tired of hearing it," he told them, rising to his feet and placing his cup back into its saucer.

The smile left Edda's face as she reached across the table and covered Benjamin's hand with her own. "Remember, Benjamin. Thee are a doctor, and thee have taken an oath to protect the sanctity of life. Being a Christian should make that commitment even stronger."

He curled his fingers around her own, squeezing reassuringly. "I hear what you are trying to say, but I will do what I have to do. So far I haven't had to resort to such extreme measures."

Edda relaxed back in her chair.

"Our prayers will follow thee, Benjamin," Jacob told him.

Smiling, Benjamin lifted his hat from the counter. "How else do you think I have made it without loss of life? Mine or anyone else's." He shook the older man's hand, his eyes suddenly grave. "You know you are taking a chance keeping the girl here? Be careful."

"God will take care of everything. When does thee think we shall see thee again?"

A small moan drifted from the other room, and Edda hurriedly pushed past them to go to the girl who was beginning to thrash about. Jacob and Benjamin followed her.

Her dark head turned restlessly against the pillow, her parched lips moving slightly.

"What is she saying?" Jacob asked his wife.

She turned shining eyes to face him. "She keeps calling for Jesus."

Benjamin smiled wryly. "When I picked her up to bring her

here, she kept saying the same thing. Maybe she thinks she's going to die."

Edda studied the tall black man from head to toe. Broad shoulders and thick muscles gave him the appearance of being more the field hand than a city doctor. Should he ever be captured, he would be considered quite a prize. "Perhaps she felt security in such strong arms," Edda told him. "Perhaps she mistook thee for the Savior."

The color of his face darkened further, and Edda knew she had embarrassed him. Jacob hastily intervened.

"When can we expect thee again?"

Benjamin watched the girl thrash about on the bed as Edda tended to her. He felt torn. Part of him wanted to stay, but he knew he had to leave. The slave coffle would be coming by any day now and he might miss it. *I might have missed it already*, he argued with himself. *Or it might not come at all. It was only a rumor*. But the girl on the bed was real, and there was a chance he could save her.

Her clothes were ragged and parts of her still dirty from lying in the mud, but there was something compelling about her. As he had carried her along, her nearness, her scent had stirred in him something as yet untouched by any woman. He wanted to stay and make sure that she would survive. Still, his conscience wouldn't allow him to forsake his mission. He had to be sure. And there was nothing that he could do that the Freemans couldn't do just as well.

Edda saw his hesitation. She rose to her feet, laying a hand against his arm. The tension in him communicated itself to her. "Go, Benjamin. Thee must. There are others depending on thee, also."

Reluctantly, he nodded his head in agreement. Turning, he quickly left the house, offering a prayer for the three people he was leaving behind.

❧

A brown column of dust rose from the road as the weary travelers trudged along. Ten male slaves were chained together, the iron bands on their necks connected by one hundred feet of chain that ran through the padlocks of each hasp. They were handcuffed in pairs, the iron staples and bolts forged to the small sections of chain linking them together at the wrists.

Three women made their way along behind the men, the white cord binding their necks stark against their dark skin. One old woman tripped, causing all three to hit the ground or be choked lifeless.

The white man riding the big roan stallion at the lead pulled his horse to a stop. Turning, he made his way to where the women were trying to scurry to their feet. Lifting the whip from his saddle, he snaked it back against the ground, ready to strike if necessary.

"Get up, and be quick about it. I ain't got all day!"

"I cain't walk no mo'," the old one moaned, and for the first time, the slave trader noticed the bleeding sores on her feet.

Face red with rage, the trader pulled his gun from his holster. "You'll walk or you'll die right here! It don't make me no never mind one way or t'other."

He pushed his hat back from his head and the women cringed in fear as they read the truth of the statement in his dark eyes.

"She be okay," one woman reassured the trader. "We okay now, ain't we, Grandma?" She turned to the now cowering woman. The older woman hastily bobbed her head up and down.

"Good." Slamming the gun back into his holster, the trader turned his horse back to the front. Ten pair of angry eyes followed his progress as he passed. Seemingly unconcerned, he cracked his whip and started them forward again.

As they rounded the bend, they found a huge tree blocking their path. It could easily be circumnavigated, but the unexpectedness of it caused the trader to pull to a stop.

"Well, I'll be. How. . . ?"

He got off his horse to inspect the tree, scratching his head in wonder. Looking around, he had no idea where the tree could have even come from. The nearest woods were at least four hundred feet away.

Suddenly a prickle of warning sent him shooting around. A huge black man stood next to his horse, cradling a rifle. He reached for his pistol, but the big man raised the rifle at the same time, pointing it right at his heart. Sweat broke out on his forehead.

"Boy, you know what'll happen to you for raisin' your hand agin a white man?"

The slow smile that spread across the giant's face did nothing toward diminishing the slaver's fear. If anything, his heart began to pound harder.

"You have the keys to these chains?" Benjamin asked, never lowering the rifle.

"Yeah, I got 'em," the trader spat, "but I ain't givin' 'em to you."

"I wasn't going to suggest that you do," Benjamin agreed softly. "You can use them yourself to open these locks, or I can allow these men to get them from your body."

Benjamin hoped that his bluff would work, because he wasn't sure he had it in him to shoot another human being, no matter how low-life they were. Not a muscle of his face showed any leniency in his attitude, however, and the trader swallowed hard.

The trader glanced briefly at the ten men standing behind the man with the gun. Ten pair of gleaming eyes promised retribution should the black man shoot him and he not die right away.

Swallowing again, the trader slowly pulled the keys from his belt. When he would have thrown them to Benjamin, he was stopped by his shaking head.

"No. You undo the chains, and make it quick. 'I ain't got all day,' " he mimicked.

The trader couldn't have been more surprised if the tree lying across the road were to get up and talk. He was only now realizing that this giant of a man talked with the same dulcet smoothness of the. . .

"You're a *Yank*!"

Benjamin grinned. "You make it sound like a curse, but I will accept it as a compliment. Indeed, I am a *Yank*, as you call it." His eyes darkened and the smile left his face. "I'm also waiting."

The threat in the words had the desired effect, and the trader hastily moved to unlock the chains. As each chain fell away, he grew more and more uneasy. Would they kill him here and now, or would they torture him? Maybe hang him?

As soon as the chain fell from one man, he shoved the trader to the side, grabbing the trader's knife from his belt. Instinct made the trader reach for the gun in his holster, but an angry voice quickly cooled the thought.

"Stop! Don't make me shoot."

When the trader turned, he was surprised to find the big man aiming the gun at the young black man holding the knife.

The man's eyes grew large. "I weren't gonna kill him." He motioned toward the women. "I'se just gonna free them."

Benjamin relaxed. "Go ahead." He turned to the trader. "You got a name?"

Face sullen, the trader hesitated. "Mercer. Shaun Mercer."

"Well, Mr. Mercer, so far so good. Let's keep it that way, shall we?" He motioned to one slave. "And you are?"

The man lifted his chin proudly. "Decker. They calls me Decker."

Nodding affirmation, Benjamin motioned to Mercer. "Decker, how about making sure Mr. Mercer here doesn't follow us."

"Huh?"

Benjamin's eyes went to the chains lying on the road. Decker's eyes followed, his brow puckered in confusion. Suddenly his face cleared and he grinned a gap-toothed grin.

Mercer was trying to decide if he should make a run for it or not. Glancing quickly around, ten pair of gleaming eyes convinced him it might not be a good idea. He allowed Decker to latch the chains to his hands and neck.

"What're you gonna do with me?"

Benjamin screwed up one side of his face as though giving the matter a great deal of consideration.

"I know what I'd like to do to 'im." The young man with the knife now cradled a young woman protectively against his side. Benjamin's eyebrows rose slightly in question.

"My name be Abe, and this here be my wife, Celine. We's from Georgia."

Benjamin was surprised. "That's a mighty long way."

Abe nodded. "Took us a long time to get no'th, but we did. Then they sent some men after us. Woulda got away, too, 'ceptin' Celine went into labor."

"Where's your baby?"

Abe and Celine glared at Mercer as tears flowed down the young woman's face. "They sold him at an auction. He say a baby just slow us down."

Sobs shook the young woman's body and her husband held her close. There were tears in his eyes as well. "We never gonna see our baby agin."

Benjamin was reluctant to assure them otherwise, but he would get as much information from them as he could and see what he could do. He had a lot of contacts.

When the group finally moved on, they left behind a spitting, snarling slave trader vowing vengeance and retribution. Benjamin had no worries about the man eventually being set free. He knew someone would come along in time, although this was a seldom used road. Fortunately for Mercer, Benjamin had a kind disposition; he left the man enough food and water for two days.

As he led the group back north, he found his thoughts continually went to the young woman at the Freemans'. Praying once again for her recovery and their safety, he firmly dislodged them from his mind. He would need all his wits about him now.

❧

Shaun Mercer lifted his head and listened intently. Was that a whistle, and was it coming this way? He listened harder. Yes, it was definitely someone whistling.

A wagon rounded the bend and came to a stop. The whistling stopped just as abruptly.

Suddenly, a figure loomed over Mercer as he lay on the ground staring up at the sky. For two days he had prayed someone would find him. Two days that seemed more like a lifetime.

"Well, can I help thee?"

Of all the stupid questions. Mercer glared upward, his eyes blinded by the sun blazing overhead.

"Can you get me outta here?"

"Well now, I don't know. Do thee have a key? How did thee manage to get thyself into this predicament?"

Mercer gritted his teeth. "I didn't git myself into this mess. Someone else did it for me, and when I get my hands on 'im. . ." He stopped, his mind finishing what his words hadn't.

"Is there a key somewhere?"

Glaring up at the person above him, Mercer could see an old man, his wide black hat pushed back from his head. *Oh great! One of them stupid, Bible-thumping, peace-loving Quakers*. He hated them almost as much as he did darkies.

"The man that trussed me up like this said he would leave the key in my horse's saddlebag."

The shadow over Mercer disappeared and the sun shone brightly in his eyes, almost blinding him. He heard the man scraping among the saddlebag, measuring his progress in his mind. He was doubtful that the big darkie had really left it.

The shadow was back and the old man knelt at Mercer's side. In a wink the chains fell from his hands and neck. Getting quickly to his feet, Mercer had to wait as a wave of dizziness assailed him. Although the darkie had left him food and water, he had been lying so long the blood fairly rushed to his head.

He found his hat next to the tree and shoved it onto his head. "Much obliged," he told the old man, for the first time able to take stock of the stranger.

Gentle blue eyes smiled back at him from a wrinkled face. "Not at all. Glad to be of service. What will thee do now?"

"Do?" Mercer snarled. "I'm going to find that skunk that left me here and hang him from the nearest tree."

The blue eyes were no longer gentle, but Mercer was too distraught to notice. Retrieving his horse, he turned to the stranger. "I'd like a tag to apply to you so that I can remember you as a friend."

The old man adjusted his hat low over his eyes and climbed back into his wagon. "The name's Jacob. Jacob Freeman."

"My thanks, Jacob. If ever you need a favor, you just ask for ole Shaun Mercer."

Wheeling the horse around, Mercer headed back north. Back where he had last seen his quarry disappear. Jacob watched him go before throwing a petition heavenward and turning his wagon back around. Benjamin had wired him just today about having found safe passage for several of the slaves. The others were still in hiding and awaiting their turn.

❧

Jenny opened her eyes slowly. She wrinkled her forehead as she became aware of the pounding pain just behind her eyes. Her throat was dry and she ran her tongue over parched lips. Where was she anyway? What had happened? Where was the sound of the river, the birds, the chattering of the squirrels she had awakened to every morning?

Hearing a sound, she tried to sit up, but her body would not respond to her commands. She lay back, trying to concentrate. Frowning only brought more pain to an already throbbing head.

She could hear someone humming and her eyes flew open. They had found her. *Oh, please, no. Don't let them take me back. Not when I was so close.*

"So, thee are awake, are thee?" a purely feminine voice asked seconds before a figure came into view. "And how are thee feeling this morning?"

Jenny frowned up at the little gray-haired lady standing over her. The kindness and compassion in her eyes sent tears to Jenny's throat. "I. . ." Her rasping voice stopped her, and she tried to clear her throat.

"Can thee tell me thy name, dear?" the woman asked, stroking Jenny's forehead softly.

Panic filled Jenny, and Edda said hastily, "It's all right. We're friends. Someone found thee and brought thee to us and we've been caring for thee. Thee has had a terrible bout with pneumonia, but it looks like thee might just mend after all. We were afraid for a while that we had lost thee."

The fear never left the brown eyes locked on the wrinkled face, but the panic subsided. Jenny glanced all around, her frightened look coming back to the old woman.

"Where am I?"

"Thee are in Kentucky. Gilbertsville, to be exact."

Jenny sighed and lay back against the soft mattress. So, she was no longer in Tennessee. She had made it to Kentucky. But what good did that do? Kentucky was a slave state, too. She had to get across the Ohio River to freedom. But how far was Gilbertsville from the river?

"There, there," the woman soothed. "Don't thee fret thy head about it. When thee are well, we'll see about getting thee to freedom." She fixed her gaze on Jenny's suspicious countenance. "Thee are a runaway, aren't thee?"

About to deny it, Jenny changed her mind. What was the use? They wouldn't believe her if she told them no.

"Can thee tell me thy name?" the woman repeated.

Jenny thought for a moment, but decided to tell the truth. After all, there were bound to be at least a dozen Jennies running around. "Jenny."

The old woman smiled. "That's a lovely name. My name is Edda. Edda Freeman."

A man joined her, his eyes twinkling merrily down at Jenny. "So. The lass is among the living, at last."

The old woman turned a smiling face to his. "This is Jenny.

Jenny, this is my husband, Jacob."

Jenny stared from one to the other, not sure what to say. These people had a peculiar way of speaking that she had never heard before and it made her reluctant to confess anything. In the end, Edda explained how their friend Benjamin would come some time in the near future and help her to freedom.

Jenny was curious about this Benjamin. She only hoped that he wasn't like Hawkins and shivered at the thought. But the Freemans were good people, and if they trusted the man, then Jenny supposed she should wait before passing judgment.

It was two more days before Jenny even felt like lifting her head. When she did, she realized that she was in a small house. There were two bedrooms, a small kitchen, and a living room. This house was not much larger than the ones Mr. Jackson had built for his workers, but this house was full of the comfort that only love can bestow.

Edda was even now busily working on a quilt of sturdy wool. She smiled when she noticed Jenny's wakefulness. Putting down the quilt, she crossed to Jenny. Laying a hand upon Jenny's forehead, she sighed. "At last. The fever has finally broken. Are thee hungry?"

Jenny realized that she was, indeed, ravenously hungry. She nodded her head, but frowned. "I don' wanna be no bother."

"My dear, thee could never be that. Shall I get thee some soup?"

"Soun's good. I'd be much obliged."

Edda helped Jenny to sit up in bed so that she could eat her food. Jenny started slow, but soon found herself gulping the delicious broth.

"Kin I ast you somethin'?"

"Certainly." Edda took the empty bowl from her and waited.

"How come. . .I heard you say. . ." Jenny frowned. "You say 'thee.' "

Edda smiled. "Jacob and I are Friends. Some people call us Quakers."

"I ain't never seen no Quakers 'fore. What is a Quaker?"

"Well, first and foremost, we are believers in God."

"Oh." The small sound sent Edda's eyebrows winging toward her gray hairline. Confused, she studied Jenny. "Are thee not a Christian?"

"Not exactly," Jenny told her, but offered no further explanation.

"But. . .but thee kept calling for Jesus when thee was ill. Over and over."

Surprised, Jenny lay back against the mattress. "I did?"

Edda nodded. "Thee even called Benjamin 'Jesus' when he carried thee here. Thee *do* know Jesus, don't thee?"

Jenny closed her eyes. "I knows Him. Least my mama do."

Edda started to say more, but she could see the girl's shoulders slumping from weariness. Pulling the covers closely about her neck, Edda left the room.

A lone tear slid down Jenny's cheek from beneath closed lids. Oh, yes. She knew Jesus. Her mama and pappy had taught her about Jesus from the time she was a babe. But now Mama and Pappy were far away, and she was lost in a strange land among strangers. True, they were kind, but they were strangers nonetheless.

Suddenly she longed for the comfort of the familiar. Were her mama and pappy all right? And had Amelia and Nate made it to safety?

Edda said she had called for Jesus in her delirium. Was she subconsciously looking for that which she steadfastly denied? If she were a praying person, she would pray for her parents and Amelia and Nate. If.

four

"Look, Jackson. All I'm askin' is that you let me search your property."

Adam Jackson crossed his arms across his chest, planting his feet firmly on the ground. He glared at Jeremiah Hawkins sitting so confidently atop his gelding. "The answer is still no."

Fire flashed briefly in the overseer's eyes before he started to slide from his saddle. "Well, maybe I'll just do it anyway."

The cocking of a pistol stopped Hawkins midway in his dismount. He slowly turned his head to encounter a revolver pointed directly at his head. His look followed the gun up the length of an arm until it came to bear on Daniel Pearson, Jackson's own overseer. Pearson's eyes were so cold Hawkins hastily remounted.

The two men glared at one another several seconds before Hawkins jerked back on the reins of his horse, turning it back toward the road. His heated glare settled on Jackson. "Mr. Greer ain't gonna be happy about this, Jackson."

"You tell Simon for me that he is welcome anytime to come and search my property. I have nothing to hide. There are no runaway slaves here. But tell him to leave his bulldog at home."

The implication of the title wasn't lost on Hawkins, lacking in intelligence as he was. His look became full of venom. "I'll get you for that, Jackson. One way or another, I'll get you for that."

Adam Jackson watched the retreating figure a moment longer before turning to the man at his side. "Bring Old Jeb to me in the study."

It wasn't more than five minutes before Pearson returned with Jenny's father. Jeb sensed that the time of reckoning was near, and his heart began to pound with trepidation.

Mr. Jackson nodded to the overseer. "Thank you, Pearson. That's all."

Jeb watched the overseer leave the room, carefully closing the door behind him. Mr. Jackson motioned for him to take a seat.

Jackson took his seat behind his desk, steepling his fingers as he leaned his elbows on the desk. Although Adam Jackson was a man of advancing years, at the age of sixty he was still a commanding presence. His gray hair was brushed smoothly back to reveal a slightly receding hairline, though for the most part his hair was lush and full. His soft blue eyes met Jeb's, and the old man read the sympathy and hurt the master couldn't disguise. Jeb swallowed hard.

"Where's Jenny, Jeb?"

Old Jeb dropped his own eyes to thc floor more from embarrassment and guilt than respect. "I don' know, Massa Jackson."

Jackson leaned back in his seat, propping his chin on his fist. "Jeb. . ."

The old man lifted his head quickly. "Honestly, Massa Jackson. I don' know."

If Adam Jackson was sure of one thing, it was the fact that this man was incapable of lying. He searched Jeb's face, his look resting on the old man's honest brown eyes. He sighed heavily.

"Tell me about it."

Jeb again dropped his look to the floor. "Jenny, she be wantin' her freedom for some time now. She talk about it a lot, but her mama and me didn't think nothin' about it."

"And what of Amelia and Nathan Greer?"

The fact that all slaves had the same last names as their masters made it sound like the two were a married couple. Jeb had to smile slightly at the irony of the situation. If possible, that would be exactly what the two would like to be, but he doubted that they would keep the name of Greer.

"Jeb?"

The words seemed to catch in the old man's throat and it took some time before he could get them past the obstruction. "Jenny. . .she. . .she disappeared the same night."

Jeb couldn't bring himself to look in the master's eyes, afraid of the condemnation he would see there. Only when he heard the chair creak did he lift his face to peer at Mr. Jackson as he rose from his seat and began to pace the floor.

"Do you know what could happen to her? Have you any idea?"

This time there was no disguising the anger that laced the words. Jackson turned to his slave, his hands clenching and unclenching at his sides. "Land sakes, man! Do you have *any* idea what could happen?"

Jeb could think of a few things, and they caused his heart to constrict within him. But then Mr. Jackson made a few more things clear that Jeb had never known. Isolated as they were on the plantation, they heard rumors from time to time, but when Jackson laid out all the laws and their consequences, the old man started to tremble.

"The Fugitive Slave Act of 1850 was meant to help owners retrieve their property," he told Jeb, his calm voice concealing his anger. "But it also was a great chance for opportunists to make a few dollars. If someone finds Jenny, they can take her captive and say that she belongs to them. Of course, it would go through the mock procedures of a court trial, but Jenny wouldn't be allowed to speak for herself, and no white man would be allowed to vouch for her. Do you understand what I'm saying, Jeb?"

Jeb was beginning to. His wide eyes sought reassurance from the man pacing before him. Jackson threw his hands up in the air.

"She could be sold to someone like Greer!"

Jeb's skin became an alarming shade lighter. "Can you do somethin', Massa Jackson?"

Jackson's look was anything but encouraging. "What, for

crying out loud? Have you any idea where I can even *begin* to look?"

Shoulders sagging in defeat, Jeb lowered his face, shaking his head negatively.

"Why didn't you tell me, Jeb?"

Again, the hurt was evident in Master Jackson's voice.

"I didn't knows what to say."

Unlike most plantation owners, Adam Jackson didn't require an accounting of the whereabouts of his slaves. The fact was, no one had ever tried to run from this plantation before. Even Pearson, the overseer, was a kind man, and because of this, the slaves worked hard and faithfully for him.

Jeb's head shot up when he felt a squeeze on his shoulder. "I understand. I only wish you would have come to me right away, then we would have had a better chance of finding her."

"I'm sorry, massa."

Jackson went to the window and stared out at the well-manicured lawn. Several seconds passed before he spoke. "I really do understand, Jeb. If it weren't for the law, I would set all my slaves free. I've tried to be a good and fair master, but even that can't substitute for freedom."

Jeb had no idea that the master even thought along those lines. It was true what Master Jackson said about being a good master. He had always been generous with his slaves where food and clothing were concerned. Even their housing was above the standard of most.

"There's nothing more I can do, Jeb. It's up to the good Lord now. All we can do is pray. Especially pray that Hawkins doesn't find her."

❧

Benjamin watched from the woods, searching for a sign from the house below him. A bright quilt hanging on the clothesline waved gaily in the brisk October breeze. A grin spread across the big man's face. Quickly he made his way toward the house, tapping lightly at the door.

Jacob Freeman opened the door, smiling when he recognized his guest.

"Benjamin! Come in! Come in!"

Benjamin smiled at Edda as she came from the kitchen wiping her hands on a towel. Her lips smiled briefly in return, but there was sadness lurking in her normally cheerful gray eyes.

Frowning, Benjamin's look went from one to the other. For a moment his heart seemed to drop to his feet. "What's wrong?" he glanced briefly about the room. "Where's the girl?"

The couple exchanged a glance before Jacob took Benjamin by the arm. "Come in and have a seat, Benjamin, and we will explain it to thee."

Impatient to hear what they had to say, Benjamin quickly seated himself on their sofa, one part of his mind registering the welcome warmth of the fire in the fireplace. October had turned chilly early, and the darkness of the sky suggested that a storm front was moving in.

"Where's the girl?" he repeated.

"She's gone."

The bald statement left Benjamin dumbfounded. "What happened?" He hardly recognized the harsh voice as his own.

"Two days ago, a man came to the door," Jacob began, but was quickly interrupted by his wife.

"I have never seen a girl so frightened. While we were talking to the man, Jenny somehow disappeared. We are not even sure which direction she took."

"Jenny?"

"That's her name."

Benjamin stood, scrubbing his hand through his hair in agitation. "Two days?"

"We had hoped that she would return," Edda told him sadly. "But she didn't."

"Thee came for her, Benjamin?" Jacob wanted to know.

Benjamin nodded his head, rubbing his hand down his neck and around to the back, where he began rubbing the knot formed by the tension of the last twenty-four hours. He had barely managed to elude a group of paddy rollers in the woods after leaving provisions for the rest of the group he was to transport. Now he arrived to find the girl missing; he had hoped to take her with the others when he went north.

"I'll go look for her. I didn't realize she was well enough to travel." His look asked the question.

"She was doing right fine," Edda assured him. "In the weeks she's been with us, she managed to gain a little weight. She's recovered completely from the pneumonia, but only the good Lord knows what will happen now."

"She'll likely head north by following the stars," Benjamin stated, his mind already formulating a plan. "If it clouds up like it looks like it's going to, she'll likely hole up somewhere until she can see the stars again."

"But Benjamin, she's had two days head start. What about the others? Thee have a responsibility to them as well," Jacob reminded.

"We can't travel in a storm. They'll be safe enough at the mill until I return."

Jacob studied Benjamin solemnly before slowly nodding his head in acquiescence. "God be with thee."

Benjamin flashed them a brief smile. "He always is."

Not wanting to waste any more time, Benjamin declined the offer of something to eat and prepared to leave. He explained briefly to Jacob how many people were waiting for transport north. Jacob promised to make sure they had food until Benjamin returned.

As Benjamin was about to leave, Edda shoved a sack into his hands. "Food," she told him. "For thee and for Jenny. Tell her. . .tell her. . ."

Benjamin understood. "I'll tell her."

"She's so lost, Benjamin. In more ways than one."

A frown creased his forehead. "But she called me Jesus." Remembering that night so many weeks ago, Benjamin was confused. The girl had continually called him Jesus in her delirium, believing herself safe in the arms of her Savior.

"It's a long story," Edda told him. "And one the lady should probably tell thee herself. Maybe she'll trust thee."

Benjamin glanced from one to the other. He could sense that there was more not being said than being said. But now was not the time to find these things out. Daylight was fast fading and Jenny would soon be on the move. Nodding briefly, he headed toward the forest to his left, which he knew would lead him north.

❧

Tilly stared through the window at fast-moving clouds, her mind a jumble of thoughts. Every night she and Jeb prayed for their errant daughter. They prayed for her safety, but most of all they prayed that the Lord would give her guidance so that she would come to know Him and His unfailing love.

Usually, they prayed before they went to bed, but this time Tilly felt an overwhelming need to go to her knees again. Climbing from the bed, she dropped to her knees in front of the now-cold fireplace. As the first rumblings of thunder stirred the night air, Tilly began her entreaty. Jenny needed her prayers. She knew it. Her mother's heart told her that her child was in desperate need of divine guidance.

She felt a presence beside her and jumped; her eyes flew open and lifted to the figure standing next to her. Her heart almost stopped beating until a familiar gravelly voice spoke to her.

"Is it Jenny?"

Tilly's breath rushed out of her as she glared at her husband. "Land sakes, old man. You scared ten years offen my life!"

Jeb knelt next to her, and taking her hand in his leathery palm, he told her, "Come on, woman. Quit yer gabbing. Our little girl needs us."

Nodding, Tilly closed her eyes and continued her petition, thankful for the reinforcement.

❧

Jenny watched the storm clouds approaching, her body trembling all over. She strained to see signs of lightning in the dark mass roiling on the horizon. Briefly the interior of the clouds was lit by what Jenny feared most: lightning.

She was in the middle of a forest surrounded by oak trees, which were notorious lightning rods. There was no place to go. Her hand shook so badly she could barely hold the small sack she had brought from the Freemans'. She had thought she was frightened when that man had come to the door looking for runaways, but it was nothing compared to the stark terror that paralyzed her mind and body now as she watched the approaching weather system.

"God, if you're out there, please turn the storm away!" She hadn't realized she had spoken aloud until a squirrel standing close to her scurried up a tree, chattering angrily down at her. So still had she been, the squirrel must have thought her part of the forest. Even now, she couldn't get her feet to move.

What was she to do? Forcing her body to listen to her mind, Jenny finally compelled her frozen limbs to go forward. Her eyes scanned each direction, hoping for some form of shelter. There was none.

Even her sky compass was obliterated by the boiling cauldron of blackness overhead.

The wind began stirring the leaves ever so slightly as the clouds approached. Before long, the limbs of the trees were whipping like an angry army on the march. Even from her relatively protected position among the dense foliage she could feel the wind increase.

The sky was suddenly illuminated by a forceful bolt of lightning, only seconds later followed by a resounding clap of thunder. Jenny threw herself to the ground, screaming with terror.

She curled herself into a ball, burying her face in her hands. When another streak of light lit the dark sky, Jenny screamed again. Her panic forced the screams from her throat in rapid succession. All other fears were crowded to the back of her mind until they ceased to exist. She never even felt when the rain began to savagely pelt her, forcing its way through the dense forest around her. The intensity of the downpour scattered the yellowed leaves from the trees, sending them showering to the ground along with the water.

When strong arms lifted her from the ground, Jenny fought mindlessly like a cornered animal against their grip. Then suddenly she remembered another time and the comfort of strong arms carrying her to safety. Her fighting ceased in an instant and she swiftly curled into the warm arms surrounding her.

Benjamin felt when Jenny's body relaxed against him. Her arms wrapped solidly around his neck and she pressed herself tightly against his chest. He could feel her lips moving against his shirt front, and bending low, he could hear her murmuring something over and over. A sudden break in the storm allowed the words to penetrate clearly through the stormy night air.

"Jesus! Jesus!"

Cupping her chin in one large hand, Benjamin forced Jenny's head back against his arm. Her eyes opened wide when she saw him, and even in the darkness he recognized the residual fear shadowing her amber-colored orbs.

Benjamin had heard her screams some distance away. Never in his life had he moved so swiftly. Even now his heart was pounding from the effort and the panic he had felt when her screams tore through the night.

"Jenny! You're all right now. You're safe with me."

Jenny gazed into ebony eyes filled with promise and felt her heart respond to the message she saw there. Her body's shaking slowed and her teeth ceased their chattering. She knew without a doubt who this man was and that she could trust him.

"Benjamin?"

Surprise filled his features before a brief smile lit his face. "Yes. I'm here to help you, Jenny. You can trust me."

She knew that already. Even though the Freemans had consistently sung this man's praises, she would have known it regardless. It was in his emotion-filled eyes, the firm timbre of his voice.

"I'm not Jesus," he told her softly, "but He sent me here to help you."

Jenny frowned and opened her mouth to protest, when another bolt of lightning struck a tree close to where they were standing. Screaming, she buried her face against his chest.

Benjamin held her close, seeking with his eyes some means of shelter. The acrid smell of charred wood assailed his nostrils. He had to get them out of here and somewhere safe. The only place he could think of was a small river not far to their right. The trees were less dense there and the ground sunk almost into a valley.

Lifting Jenny into his arms, he began striding rapidly toward his destination. He had almost reached it, when the wind suddenly died down and the rain ceased. The sky was still dark around them, but things had grown eerily quiet. Even the night animals were not to be heard.

Suddenly, in the distance, Benjamin heard a loud rumbling. He hadn't heard that sound very often, but he knew what it meant even if he couldn't see it in the dark.

"Dear God!"

Jenny heard the soft exclamation meant, she was sure, to be a prayer. The distant sound hadn't registered with her at first, but now she could hear it growing louder as it moved closer. The trees began to sway around them, their movement growing more furious as the wind increased. A tornado!

Benjamin dropped her to her feet, grabbed her by the hand, and started running. More terrified than ever, Jenny followed meekly where he led. She had no idea where they could run to escape the raging monster following them. There was nowhere to go, and she had almost resigned herself to dying. Already the trees were billowing toward the ground. Limbs began to snap as the roar from the twister increased. They had no way of knowing if they were moving in the right direction to avoid it.

They broke from the trees, and Benjamin gave a loud cheer as he continued toward the river. Wondering at his purpose, Jenny would have balked, but Benjamin gave her no chance. He jerked her forward, almost making her lose her balance.

She continued to stumble along in his wake, certain that

they were about to die. The force of the vortex was pulling her backward as Benjamin continued to pull her forward.

Then Jenny could see what he had been seeking. A small dip in the ground formed a natural overhang, and Benjamin hurried them toward it. Shoving Jenny in ahead of him, Benjamin then threw his body across hers.

Seconds later, trees pummeled the earth around them, the roaring of the twister deleting all other sound. Jenny covered her ears with her hands, biting her lip until she could taste blood. A large tree crashed across the hole where they lay, but they were sheltered by the groove in the earth. Buried under the tree, they were protected from flying debris as the storm raged around them.

As suddenly as it began, it was over. Benjamin continued to hold the trembling Jenny long after the tornado had passed. Her whimpering touched a chord deep inside him that had never been reached before. He wanted to protect her. Reassure her. Promise her safety. But he knew that might not be possible. Still, he would do all in his power to make it so.

Jenny felt Benjamin lift himself away from her in preparation to leaving their shelter. She clung harder to his shirt, not wanting to abandon the protection of their little cave. He pried her hands loose from his shirt front and held them tucked within his own large hands.

"Jenny, we have to leave. We can't stay here."

She heard the words, but their message failed to convey itself to her still-frightened mind.

"Jenny," he crooned. "Jenny, we have to go."

Slowly reason returned. Jenny lifted her face to the night sky and watched for traces of lightning. None were there, only the steady rhythmic pelting of the rain that was beginning to chill her to the bone.

Benjamin climbed from beneath the tree, pulling Jenny out after him. He held her close for a brief time, then suddenly fell to his knees. With a small cry, Jenny dropped beside him, clutching his arm.

"Benjamin! Are you hurt?"

"No," he told her softly, and then he bowed his head and began to pray.

"Merciful God of Heaven! Thank You for Your protection. Thank You for helping me to find Jenny, and please, Lord, help us to return safely. In Jesus' holy name."

When Benjamin's eyes met Jenny's, she was startled by the intensity of the light she saw there. She stared in wonder at the shine of glory reflected in his eyes.

Getting swiftly to his feet, Benjamin reached for Jenny's hand and lifted her to his side. He wanted to sing hallelujahs to the Lord. It was almost more than he could stand to keep it within. God had shown him the way and protected Jenny and himself even from the power of nature. He was awed and humbled.

He was even more awed when he looked about them and saw the massive destruction of the forest around them. The storm had cut a swath at least two hundred yards wide. The area around them was a tangle of shrubs and trees. Amid all this destruction, God had sheltered them.

Taking Jenny's hand, he began walking away from the river and back through the woods, or what was left of it. His whole being was flooded with his wonder and thanksgiving to God as the blood surged furiously through his veins. He would never forget this night as long as he lived.

Jenny followed behind, not certain of their destination but not really caring. She somehow expected Benjamin to get her safely to freedom. The Freemans had practically guaranteed it. But more than that, she was just plain weary. Benjamin seemed to have enough faith in God for the both of them, so she would just let Him prove Himself through Benjamin. For the first time in her life, her Ashanti blood was subdued and she was willing to be told what to do.

Before long she realized that they were headed back in the same direction Jenny had traversed over the last couple of days. She jerked her hand from Benjamin's and came to an abrupt halt. "You're going the wrong way!"

Surprised, Benjamin tried to read her face in the dark. "We're going back to the Freemans'."

Jenny began shaking her head. "I done traveled two days no'th and I ain't goin' back now."

"Listen, Jenny. I'll help you get to freedom, but there are some other people I need to take with us. I left them in the Freemans' millhouse and they're waiting for me."

Jenny was resolute. There was no way she was going to backtrack after two days.

"You haven't come as far as you might think," Benjamin told her. "We can be back at the Freemans' by tomorrow night."

Astounded, she began shaking her head. "That cain't be right."

Benjamin's lips tugged into a small grin. The woman looked like a helpless child standing there defying him in her wide-eyed innocence.

"You traveled in circles for some time. That's why I was able to catch up with you so quickly."

Jenny remembered the time when she had become hopelessly lost. It had seemed an eternity at the time, but eventually she had glimpsed the North Star through a small break in the clouds and had been able to continue on her way. And now this big ox wanted to take her back! Not if her life depended on it.

Benjamin could tell Jenny was struggling with the decision. He moved closer to her in the darkness. Unerringly, his hands found her shoulders.

"Jenny, there are people depending on me. I can help you, too. Believe me, it will take you less time going back to the Freemans' and going forward with me than traipsing through the woods of Kentucky alone. I can make your way much easier."

Jenny's suspicions were rising. She peered at him through the darkness, not able to discern his dark features in the dimness. "You don' sound like no darkie."

She could see his teeth flash briefly in the dark. "Well, I am. I just happen to be an educated one."

Trying to see his face in the darkness was impossible. Jenny moved closer, bumping into his chest. Placing her hands there, she tried to focus on his face, although she really couldn't see it. Only an outline. She could feel his heart begin to thunder against her palms and heard his quick intake of breath. There was something undefinable that passed between them, causing Jenny's own heart to race in response to his. Suddenly, he dropped his hands from her shoulders and moved away from her.

"I can tell you all about me on the way," he told her, his voice hoarse. "Will you come with me?"

Jenny looked forward through the trees that she knew led north. She knew that tornadoes move in a northeasterly direction, and the storm had providentially cut a swath in that direction. There was no telling how many miles the tornado could have gone. She would have a fairly clear strip to travel.

She looked behind Benjamin and saw where the storm had come from. Did she want to go back? She shook her head. She was just so bone weary, it was hard to think straight.

"Jenny?"

She stared at Benjamin's outstretched hand. It would be so nice to have someone look out for her. Reflections of the Freemans' faces as they related stories about this man passed through her mind. Their voices had been filled with respect, honor, and yes, even love. Suddenly, her doubts dwindled until she was left with a restless longing that she couldn't explain.

From the time she was born, there had always been someone to give her directions: the Jacksons, Mr. Pearson, her parents; but she hadn't heeded their advice or listened to their wisdom. More than once her own independent nature had caused her problems. That was one reason she shied away from following after the white man's God. Well, maybe it was time for a change. After what she had witnessed this night, she had some serious thinking to do.

Always a decisive person, for the first time she was lost in a sea of uncertainty. Slowly she lifted her hand and placed it in Benjamin's larger, stronger one. His fingers closed warmly around her own.

Benjamin squeezed her fingers reassuringly, his teeth flashing in the darkness. She could feel his approval even from a distance. Hoping she was doing the right thing, she allowed him to lead her back the way she had come. Deeper into the slave state of Kentucky.

five

They traveled all night, and Jenny was glad for the cover of darkness, not only to escape detection, but also to avoid what she knew the morning light would bring.

As red streaks of dawn formed above the ever-lightening band of twilight, both Jenny and Benjamin had to stop, their eyes wide with shock. For as far as the eye could see, scattered debris lay strewn around them. Huge trees were snapped close to the ground with the power of the twister—or twisters—that had hit the night before. The evidence was there that more than one demon had been spawned during the storm.

For the first time, Jenny was able to actually *see* her rescuer. As she followed close in his wake, she noticed broad shoulders tapered to a lean waist. She could hardly believe that the man striding along before her was a doctor from the city and not some field hand. His hair curled tightly against his scalp in a close cut, unlike many of the slaves she was used to seeing.

When he finally stopped and turned to make a remark, she was able to see his face for the first time. Her breath caught in her throat. He was unlike any man she had ever seen before. The size of him was similar to others, but a fire was in his eyes that was a clear contrast to the apathy and hopelessness of those she was used to. There was something so *alive* about him.

He was studying her as thoroughly as she was studying him. She knew she must look a sight, but frankly, she just didn't care.

He reached out and plucked a small stick from her hair, twisting it in his fingers before dropping it to the ground.

"How are you holding up?" he wanted to know.

She was still amazed to hear him talk. So educated. The

tones so honeyed. It made her afraid to speak, almost. She was intensely curious about him.

"I'se fine," she told him, turning her head away so he couldn't see her cheeks darkening with color. "How much longer?"

"Not long now. We'll reach the millhouse before we reach the Freemans'."

Suspicious, she stayed put as he began to move forward. "What's at the millhouse?"

He stopped and came back to where she still stood. His face was serious, but there was humor lurking in his mahogany eyes. "I told you that I have others to transport. They're waiting for me there."

Jenny did remember him saying something to that effect. Her eyes narrowed; forgetting her earlier confidence in the man, she stood still, trying to decide if she could really trust him. Although there weren't many, there were some blacks who sold information to the whites about runaway slaves. It was incomprehensible to her that someone as educated as this man, already free in the North, would make trips to the South to help runaway slaves. Of course it was just as inconceivable that a black man could speak the way this one did, yet she could not deny the evidence. Still, his whole bearing, his very manner made her leery.

He took her hand and she again felt the potency of his touch. Jerking away, she moved forward on her own. She could hear him sigh as he moved into step behind her.

"Why don't I tell you a little about myself? Maybe you would feel more trusting then."

She doubted it, but she *was* curious to know more about him. Shrugging her shoulders, she left it for him to decide.

"Well, let's see. Is there anything in particular you want to know?"

Jenny didn't hesitate. "How'd you 'scape, and where'd you 'scape from?"

"I've never been a slave. My home has always been in

Philadelphia." His voice was so soft, she thought she had misunderstood him.

"They got slaves in Philadelphia, too?"

He shook his head. "No, Jenny. Pennsylvania outlawed slavery long ago."

She stopped in her tracks, her eyes wide with wonder. "Is Pennsylvania in Canada?"

For a moment Benjamin stared into her eyes large with bewilderment and forgot what they were talking about. Of all the people he had transported over the past few years, none had affected him as much as this one woman had.

"No, Pennsylvania is part of the United States. It's one of the oldest states. Surely you knew there were free states. Isn't that where you were headed?"

She shook her head vehemently. "No, suh. I's headed for Canada." She frowned, her eyes wandering over him as she tried to form her next question. "How long you been free?"

Placing his hand at her back, he nudged her into a walk. "I've always been free. So was my father before me."

He could see her struggle to comprehend what he was telling her. "You thought *all* blacks were freed slaves?"

She nodded. "Ain't that so?"

Benjamin realized that Jenny must have spent her entire life on a plantation. Any news of the outside world was rare, because plantation masters were afraid to allow it for fear of an uprising. If slaves thought all states were as harsh as southern states, they would have no reason to try to run away. The known was preferable to the unknown. He grew more curious.

"What made you decide to run away, Jenny? Where were you going?"

"No'th."

Lips twitching, Benjamin tried again. "But where north? What were you going to do when you got there?"

She shrugged, but he noticed the droop to her shoulders. "I don' know. I was just goin'." She glanced at him briefly. "If you wasn't a slave, how'd you git to this country?"

"My father was from England. He came here seeking a better way of life, just like most colonists. England abolished slavery many years ago, and all blacks in England are free today. Many stay. Many come here seeking their fortunes."

Her dark brows wrinkled into a confused frown. "They come here *willingly*? They not slaves?"

Benjamin's brows formed a straight line across his forehead as he contemplated how best to explain things to Jenny.

"There are many blacks in England who have families here in the States. Their family lines were established long before the Revolutionary War, when blacks came here as indentured servants."

"Is that like a slave?"

Benjamin could tell that she had a quick mind. "Kind of, except that it's a contract where one person agrees to serve another. At the end of the time agreed upon, the servant is free. Many of the first blacks to this country were indentured servants, along with many whites."

Jenny struggled to keep pace with his steps, her eyes growing wide at this new information. "White slaves?"

Benjamin's voice drifted back over his shoulder. "Indentured servitude is an agreement by *both* people. It isn't forced. And then the document spells out the particular duties of both servant and owner. When the end of the contract comes, the servant is free and goes his own way. Usually the contract requires the owner to give compensation to the servant so that he has at least *some* money to live on until he can get started."

Jenny studied the man striding ahead of her, so confident, so intelligent, and felt suddenly very inadequate. How did a person, a *black* person, get to be that way? Education had always been beyond her grasp, no matter how she hungered for it. To her, education meant power, and that power was denied to her people. How had this man come by his? She really wanted to know.

"How'd you git to be a doctor?"

"I went to school for it."

Jenny stopped dead in her tracks. It took a moment for Benjamin to realize that she wasn't following, and he returned to her. He sighed with exasperation. "Jenny, we're never going to get to the millhouse at this rate."

She pulled back from him, her eyes suddenly blazing dangerously. "You'se lying! It's agin the law to educate blacks."

His voice was reassuringly low and soothing. "Not in the North."

Although he could sympathize with her confusion, he hadn't time to waste. Taking her firmly by the hand, he began pulling her along. At first she resisted, but when she could no longer fight him, she unwillingly allowed herself to be dragged along. Her plantation training warred with her thirst for freedom. So conditioned had she been to obey, she found herself yielding when she wasn't certain that she should.

As they walked, Benjamin kept up a running dialogue describing life in the North and its advantages. Although Jenny wasn't entirely convinced of his credibility, she nevertheless found herself beginning to relax her guard. Question followed question, until Jenny's curiosity, though far from being satisfied, was at least appeased.

The woods were thinning now and in the distance a clearing appeared. A large cotton field shone white in the morning light. Here there were no traces of last night's rampaging tempest.

At the far edge of the field a modest structure gleamed, a large wheel moving slowly at its side. Benjamin headed them through the cotton field straight for the small building that Jenny could see was a millhouse like the one Mr. Jackson had on his property. As they drew closer, the sound of water could be heard rushing swiftly, its puny waters having been increased by last night's rainwater until it was a mighty stream.

Moving silently, Benjamin pulled Jenny along after him until they were standing before a well-tended door. He knocked twice, then knocked twice again.

Faint shuffling could be heard from the other side of the portal until finally a quavery voice asked, "Who there?"

"A friend with a friend," Benjamin answered.

Slowly the door creaked open on its solid hinges, and a frightened black face appeared. A sudden smile lit the dark man's features when he recognized Benjamin. Pulling the door wider, he rapidly motioned them inside.

Jenny was reluctant to enter the dark interior, but Benjamin gave her no time to decide. He tugged her hand, pulling her in and closing the door behind them.

Jenny's eyes needed a moment to adjust, but when they did, she noticed shadows moving within the building. She felt the hair rise on the back of her neck.

Benjamin released her and went to a corner, where he pulled a lamp from a small cupboard. After lighting it, he lifted it above eye level and searched the room.

"Where's Lila?"

A shadow moved from behind a stack of grain bags. "I'se here."

Another shadow moved to the woman's side. "I'se here, too, Mr. Ben."

In all, there were six other people in the little millhouse, besides Jenny and Benjamin. As Jenny looked at each, one thing became perfectly clear. Although there was fear in their eyes, there was also hope.

Benjamin motioned to Jenny. "This is Jenny. She'll be coming with us. Why don't you tell her your names."

They nodded at Jenny as one by one they introduced themselves. Lila, obviously pregnant, was married to Bill. Both had fled when their master had decided to sell Bill to another plantation owner farther south. Periodically Lila would rub her swollen abdomen, a grimace slicing across her features. Jenny wondered if her time was near, her heart sinking at the prospect. She had allowed herself the luxury of depending on a man she barely knew to get her to freedom, and she wouldn't allow anything to stand in her way. If this pregnant woman slowed them down, Jenny would just have to strike out on her own.

Jasper was just a boy, though at the age of sixteen, Jenny assumed he could be considered a man. His size portended a future giant. He dropped his head shyly when they were introduced.

Annie was two years younger than Jasper, but they were no relation. Annie's eyes constantly strayed toward the young man's location, and Jenny wondered if something was transpiring between them. They didn't volunteer the information of their origination, and Jenny didn't ask.

Dawson was a middle-aged man, shoulders bowed with years of toil and misery. He was going north since his wife had been sold and had disappeared, and he felt he had no reason to live. The fanatical light in his eyes worried Jenny.

Last, but not least, was old Zeke, Bill's father. He reminded Jenny so much of her own pappy that she felt tears crowd into her throat. Although he was stooped with age, the friendly light in his dark eyes made one want to draw closer to him. Wisdom spoke to her from the depths of his soft gaze. If she were to trust anyone besides Benjamin, it would be this man.

Jenny offered no information regarding herself and she could see the uncertainty in the others' eyes. Turning to Benjamin, she asked, "What now?"

He pulled up a small stool and the others crowded close around him. "I think now would be a great time to move. The tornado last night caused so much destruction, I doubt anyone will be concerned about escaping slaves for a time. Still, I don't want to chance moving in the daylight, so we'll wait until dark." His look focused on Jenny briefly before he turned away. "Try to get some sleep. It's going to be a long night."

Nodding in agreement, they all moved away to find a place to accommodate themselves for the remainder of the day. Benjamin went to the cupboard and returned with some biscuits and slices of ham. He handed them to Jenny, who made no move toward taking them. Instead her eyes lifted to his in inquiry.

He smiled. "The Freemans make sure that passengers have food and shelter."

Jenny's stomach rumbled at that instant and her face darkened in embarrassment. She reached for the food, but her eyes were held by Benjamin's.

"Passengers?" she asked softly.

He shrugged. "Words we use for the Underground Railroad. I'm a conductor. The Freemans are a station."

"I ain't never rode no train," Jenny told him through mouthfuls of biscuit.

Benjamin smiled. "In time, Jenny. All things in time."

She watched him walk over and bend down to talk to Lila and Bill, wondering just what he had meant by that comment. He placed his hand against Lila's swollen stomach. Even from that distance, Jenny could see the worry lines etch his face.

She jumped when someone touched her on the shoulder. Glancing up, she found Annie holding a glass filled with water.

Jenny took the water, her eyes dropping to her lap. She was in an uncomfortable situation and knew of nothing to say to this young girl. "Thanks," she finally managed. After a minute, Annie left her and Jenny sighed with relief.

Placing the now-empty glass on the floor next to her, Jenny lay down and feigned sleep. Her mind tumbling from one direction to another wouldn't let her relax, but she knew she would have to be rested for the arduous journey tonight.

With uncanny insight, Jenny knew that someone was watching her. Her heart began to race a little faster as she shifted her position on the blanket. Perhaps it was just her imagination, but she didn't think so. Finally, curiosity got the best of her and her eyes seemed to fly open of their own accord.

Benjamin sat against the far wall, his gaze fixed firmly on Jenny. She surprised a look on his face that was there and then instantly gone. It was possible that she had imagined that look, but she doubted it and her palms grew sweaty in response.

Their eyes stayed locked together for some time, probing, assessing. Never before had Jenny felt the conflict of feelings that Benjamin engendered in her. Deliberately turning away, Jenny closed her eyes and willed herself to sleep.

❧

Benjamin could tell when Jenny's breathing turned from consciousness to that of deep sleep. Unable to help himself, he let his eyes wander over her from head to toe. He felt drawn to her for some reason, and he couldn't for the life of him figure out why. Several women had caught his interest before, but it had been a passing fancy, and his attention had quickly waned. He firmly believed God had a life mate chosen especially for him. Someone to share his thoughts, his work. He was doubtful that it could be someone like Jenny.

Truth be told, she wasn't much to look at. Her clothes were torn and dirty, and mud smudged her face and arms. Her cornrow braids were also littered with leaves and brush, but over and above that, Jenny had an elemental quality about her that tempted a man's mind. And he was no exception. He wondered what she would look like cleaned up and dressed properly.

As often as he had helped passengers to freedom, never once had he been as enamored of a woman as he seemed to be of this one. Like most slaves, Jenny seemed to guard her thoughts and feelings jealously. He longed to look into her mind, to know just what her thoughts were.

What had she endured in her life of bondage? There were no stripes on her back like those of others he had tended; that was the one thing that stood out clearly to him when he had treated her pneumonia. Yet knowing her the short time he had, he knew she was no docile, cowed servant. What was her story, then?

Annie sat down beside him, her white teeth flashing. Benjamin knew the young girl was infatuated with him, but he also knew that it came more from the romantic notion of a knight in shining armor than anything else. She saw him as some kind of hero.

He returned her smile, careful to keep his distance. "You should be asleep, Annie," he told her.

"I cain't sleep, Uncle Benjamin. I'se all sleeped out."

Benjamin's lips twitched into a grin, as much from Annie's unique vocabulary, as from her calling him "uncle." It was normal for younger black children to call elder blacks "uncle" or "aunt" as a sign of respect, but at times it made him feel extremely old. "Try, okay? We all need to be rested for tonight."

"You'se ain't sleeping," she told him slyly, her eyes sliding to Jenny's sleeping form.

For the first time, Benjamin realized that others were watching him as closely as he had been watching Jenny. One eyebrow lifted upward as his gaze slid to the young girl by his side.

"Annie, you're a rather impertinent young girl."

Her smile was replaced by a frown. "Huh?"

Benjamin tweaked her nose. "Never mind. Now go get some sleep."

The authority in his voice was not to be denied, and as with Jenny, Annie's training had her hurriedly moving from his side and across the room. Benjamin refrained from further contemplation of Jenny's sleeping form, much as he was tempted. Instead, he moved silently about the room, packing things in readiness for tonight's move.

A knock on the door sent shadows scurrying in every direction. It still amazed Benjamin when passengers moved with such wraithlike stealth. He listened for the second knock. Only then did he move from his own frozen position.

"Who's there?"

"A friend," came the soft response.

Benjamin unlatched the door and Jacob Freeman slipped inside. His eyes quickly scanned the interior before lighting upon Jenny, who was just rising from her pallet. The wan look of her features suggested just how tired she was.

"Thee found her," Jacob exclaimed with satisfaction.

Jenny climbed to her feet and hesitantly smiled at the old man. He returned her smile.

"We were worried about thee."

"I'se sorry, Mr. Freeman. I just gots so scared, I ran."

"I understand," he agreed. His look returned to Benjamin. "I need to speak to thee. Will thee come outside a moment?"

Benjamin could feel Jenny's suspicious gaze riveted on his back. He closed the door behind them, blinking rapidly against the bright sunlight.

"What is it, Jacob?"

The old man turned, and Benjamin was suddenly arrested by the intensity in his blue eyes.

"Thee has to move tonight."

Frowning, Benjamin studied the other man's face. "I intended to. What's happened?"

At a slight rustle, both men froze. Suddenly, a rabbit lunged from the cover of the cotton and scurried to the river, never noticing the two silent men until the last moment. It was almost comical the way the little animal skidded to a halt, scrambling to turn himself around.

Jacob released his breath slowly. "It seems that several plantations in the area were hit hard by the twisters and that several slaves decided to take the opportunity to use that to their advantage. So far, they are farther south, but they'll for sure be coming this way. Thee should leave as soon as it's dark enough."

Benjamin placed his large hands on his hips, studying the terrain around him. "I know you're right," he began hesitantly, "but I'm almost inclined to wait and see if there are others I could help. Surely it wouldn't take long for them to get this far."

Jacob was already shaking his head. "That's foolish talk. Thee knows if some make it here, we'll hide 'em till thee can return. We'll send thee a message. But right now, thee has others to worry about, and it's possible the searchers will get here before any slaves." He frowned at the rapidly flowing stream. "It's just as likely that with them hunters trailing along in these woods, they'll come upon all of you. Maybe thee should just sit tight."

"No," Benjamin disagreed. "We need to put as much distance as we can between us and the trackers. We'll leave as soon as it's dark."

Heaving a sigh, Jacob slapped Benjamin's back in understanding. "I thought thee might say that." He strode to the corner of the building and pulled a large sack from beside it. Coming back to Benjamin, he handed him the sack. "Edda says to stay well, and never forget that our prayers are with thee."

Benjamin's concerned eyes meshed with his friend's. "I'm worried, Jacob. I have a woman about to give birth and a man with a yearning to die. I could certainly use all the prayers you can spare."

Blue eyes twinkled reassuringly back at him. "Thee has got 'em. Remember, Benjamin, that God is in control. Whatever happens, we have to always believe that."

Benjamin watched Jacob wade through the white cotton until his form was swallowed up by the forest. Already Benjamin's heart was racing with the realization that he would soon have to move these passengers from this location through a woods that might be swarming with trackers.

He returned to the interior of the millhouse and continued his preparations to leave. After several moments of debating with himself, he decided to keep the information of the escaped slaves to himself.

When he glanced up, he found Jenny's gaze, clouded with uncertainty, locked on him. He tried to reassure her with his own look, but she turned away and lay down on the blanket on the floor. No one else seemed to be bothered by his exchange, but the tension emanating from Jenny was almost palpable.

Why was she so distrusting of him? Their skin was the same color, yet for some reason, Jenny seemed to have set him apart. Maybe it had to do with the fact that he had never been a slave. Or maybe the things he had told her seemed so unreal that she thought he was being deceitful.

He wanted her to trust him, but quite frankly, he didn't know how to accomplish that.

six

Benjamin studied the waning crescent in the sky and sighed with satisfaction. In two days' time there would be a new moon, which meant complete darkness except for the stars glowing in that dark expanse of night sky. The next week would be the best time to travel, and with any luck—or he supposed he should say "Providence"—he would have these people well on their way to freedom.

The storm had cooled temperatures dramatically, and already his fellow travelers were shaking with chills. If not for the extra clothing and blankets that the Freemans had provided, they would now be in even worse shape. A frown wrinkled his forehead as they trudged along the still sodden ground. If he was not mistaken, and he doubted that he was, Lila would have a new son or daughter by tomorrow night. That would certainly throw a kink into the works, but it wouldn't be insurmountable. At least he hoped not.

The silence among the woods was eerie in the semi-light from the moon. The only sound was the crackling of the dense underbrush as they made their way forward. Suddenly, an owl screeched from somewhere to his left, and at the sound Annie unexpectedly threw herself to the ground screaming, her head buried beneath her arms. For a moment, everyone froze in fear, not knowing what had transpired.

Jasper tried to lift the young girl from the ground, all the while whispering soft words of encouragement, but the girl would not be budged.

"It's the death messenger," she wailed. "We's all gonna die!"

Over the past several years, Benjamin had had plenty of opportunity to come in contact with many of the southern superstitions. For this one, there was a simple solution, and although as a Christian he tried to refrain from giving in to such mumbo jumbo, he dropped his pack and quickly knelt beside the still moaning girl. He prayed fervently that no trackers were close by, or he was in serious trouble. Annie's screams would have alerted anyone within at least a mile radius.

"It's okay, Annie," he told her soothingly. "I know what to do."

Rising to his feet, Benjamin lifted his hands chest level, joining the two little fingers of his hands. He then lifted the joined fingers higher in the direction he had heard the owl and began pulling as though to pull them apart. He would explain the futility of such shenanigans to the girl later, but right now the only way to appease her hysteria was to go along with the things she believed. Feeling foolish, he nonetheless continued his finger choking motion until he could see Annie slowly lift her head from her folded arms.

She stared with fascination into the darkness. When no other sound came from the direction of the woods he was pointing, her lips turned up into a tremulous smile.

"You did it, Uncle Benjamin. You choked the spirit. Now he cain't hurt us no more."

Finally allowing herself to be helped to her feet, Annie clung to Jasper, her body still trembling. This was the one thing that Benjamin had had to fight, against which he felt helpless. When someone had faith in something, it was not easy to sway them otherwise. These people needed to replace their superstitions with the love and peace of Jesus Christ. Only then would they be truly free. Too often whites had used these superstitions against them to keep them enslaved. Even other blacks had been known to use such things to maintain a hierarchy among the slaves.

Digging in the sack he carried, Benjamin produced a small lantern from its depths. He struck a match, and before long a small circle of light surrounded them. Taking a deep breath, he told them, "Stay close, and keep your voices low." His look fixed pointedly on Annie, causing the girl to draw even closer against Jasper's side.

As they started on their way again, Jenny moved into step beside Benjamin. She was not surprised at the way he had handled the situation. As devoted a Christian as her own mother was, she still held to many of the superstitions on which she had been raised.

"Can I ask you something?"

His smile left her momentarily rattled. It unnerved her to have such a reaction to the man. There was a radiance about him that reached out to her even through the darkness. Even his eyes gleamed with a peculiar light that made her want to somehow grasp what he unknowingly offered.

"What did you want to ask me?"

Not fully alert, Jenny chose that moment to trip over a jutting tree root. Benjamin grabbed her, waiting until he knew she had regained her balance before releasing her.

More flustered than ever, Jenny pulled as far from him as space permitted. Brushing at imaginary leaves, she avoided his eyes until her breathing returned to normal. If anyone had told her just a few days ago that a man's touch would send her into a spin, she would have laughed in their face. But now . . .well now she didn't consider it a laughing matter.

"If you a Christian, how come you used magic to choke a spirit?"

Benjamin glanced around at the others following close in their wake. Each face registered a hint of awe and more than a little fear. He would have consequences to face from his earlier actions; he should have known better than to compromise his beliefs in such a way. He offered a quick prayer of apology to the Lord, and sighing, he turned back to watching a trail that few eyes could see.

"I didn't use magic, Jenny. I used common sense. Obviously we startled the owl when we came into his territory. I assumed that like most animals, he would flee the premises when intruders trespassed."

When Benjamin finally glanced at her, he was unprepared

for the utter astonishment on her features. His brows drew together. "What?"

"You sounds just like Miss Adelaide's tutor!" she told him, her voice filled with admiration.

Relieved that she was more impressed with his speech than his magical abilities, he smiled broadly. "Is that bad?"

"Even the masters don' speak that. . .that. . ."

"The term is educated," he filled in for her. "And given time, you will be able to speak the same way."

Jenny shook her head, tilting it impishly. "I don' rightly knows that I *want* to talk like that. My people choose to speak the way they do, cause. . .well. . ."

She paused and he could see her struggling for a way to make him understand. Benjamin was beginning to think that he was destined to finish her sentences for her. "Because it gives them a feeling of unity?"

She nodded, relieved that he did, indeed, understand. "Yeah. I s'pose."

Referring back to their original conversation, Benjamin tried once again to make Jenny appreciate what he had tried to accomplish with Annie. "I don't believe in magic," he stressed. "The only magic I believe in is God's ability to wash away our sins with the blood of His Son."

Unconvinced, she raised an eyebrow dubiously. "Then why you pretend to do magic?"

Benjamin sighed. "It was the only thing that I could think of at the time that would stop Annie's hysterics. I'll explain things to her later, but right now we're still too close to the area the hunters are searching."

Jenny's eyes flittered around quickly, the stiffness of her carriage emphasizing her returning anxiety. "Do you think they heard her?"

"It's possible, but I hope not. Still, I would feel more comfortable if we could put as much distance between us and this area as possible."

He picked up their pace slightly, and Jenny continued by

Benjamin's side until the brush became too dense for two abreast. Dropping behind him, she studied him as he walked along.

He intrigued her. Never had she known a black man with such confidence. She wondered if Nat Turner had been such a man. Although the whites had tried to keep the information from reaching the slaves, the renegade slave had become something of a hero among the blacks. Not that she approved of his murdering forty white people, but after some of the things she had heard, she could understand his insanity. On the other hand, she couldn't imagine Benjamin instigating such a rebellion. For all of his size, there was an unusual gentleness about him, but she knew from experience that it was tempered with steel.

As the night progressed, the darkness increased until they could barely see their hands in front of their faces even with the lamplight. Each person clung to the person in front of him, making traveling difficult. Finally, Benjamin came to a stop.

Although Benjamin had said nothing, Jenny could sense they were at a particularly dangerous section of their journey. It was in the very way he walked, his eyes continually going from left to right, shoulders tense, hands gripping the rifle he held clenched in his hand. She wanted to ask questions, but she knew this was not the time.

Before long they came upon a thin dirt road that was more like a path among the dense brush. Benjamin lifted the glass of the lantern and blew out the flame. Suddenly, they were plunged into total, inky darkness. Jenny could hear Annie's whimpers coming from behind.

"Listen to me." The sibilant hiss came as a disembodied voice from the surrounding gloom, and Jenny shuddered. "This section of the woods is patrolled by paddy rollers. I don't want to hear a sound from any of you. I won't have everyone jeopardized because of one person's fears. Jasper, do whatever you have to do to make sure Annie controls herself."

The warning was clear. Annie's whimpers ceased. After

telling each person to hold tightly to the person in front of him, Benjamin once again moved forward. Looking carefully both ways, he led them stealthily across the road and re-entered the forest on the other side.

Each crackle of brush seemed to resound throughout the forest with a deafening intensity. Even their breathing sounded loud until it mingled with the rising wind.

How long they traveled, Jenny had no idea, but suddenly Benjamin called a halt. He once again lit the lantern and a collective sigh of relief came from the group as the small circle of light surrounded them once again.

"In just a few hours, it will be daylight," he told them, his whisper only slightly louder than before. "There's another station about fifteen miles from here that I hope to make before then."

"How far are we from the river?" Zeke wanted to know.

Not for several hours had Benjamin been able to take stock of his companions. Now he noticed the lines of fatigue etched around the old man's mouth. Although he had to be exhausted, Zeke hadn't complained once.

"Not far," Benjamin answered. "We should make the river by tomorrow night."

"Then what?" Dawson asked, his eyes shimmering eerily in the soft lantern light.

"Then we cross into Illinois."

Jenny, who had wearily dropped to the nearest log, came swiftly to her feet. "Illinois?"

Benjamin nodded. "Illinois is just across the river from where we will be going. The current of the river will take us several miles downstream before we reach the other side. After we reach Illinois, we'll cross east through Indiana and then north to Canada. Traveling through Indiana is the best way to go because we can travel in daylight."

"How so?" Old Zeke asked, clearly puzzled.

Smiling, Benjamin told them, "In Indiana, a black man is considered free unless proven otherwise. Still, we'll have to be careful of unscrupulous slavers looking for black people to claim as slaves so they can carry them south and resell them. Now, if everyone's rested enough, we need to try to make the next station before daylight. This is dangerous territory because the slavers know this is the last chance they have to catch slaves freely."

In the end, it was long after first light before Benjamin found the cave he was looking for. He hurried the others inside, carefully scrutinizing the surrounding terrain before following. Everyone refused to move past the entrance until he came in carrying the glowing lantern. The dim light was swallowed by the immense size of the hole in the ground. Water could be heard trickling from somewhere beyond the lantern's glow.

As Benjamin moved farther into the cavern, the others followed slowly. Jenny was almost certain they would have preferred facing the paddy rollers to descending into the dark recess. She shivered at the chill, damp air but was heartened to see several crates and pieces of furniture within the cavern's immense interior. The obvious signs of habitation gave her a slight feeling of security.

Benjamin found several other lanterns among the sparse furnishings. After lighting them, he placed them strategically around the area until a small room was formed. The others huddled within the light's confines, fearful of the darkness beyond.

A pile of sticks lay ready, and all Benjamin had to do was set a match to the dry wood. Before long, a cheerful fire blazed, relieving the cave of some of its chill. Shadows flashed in weird moving patterns along the stone walls.

Zeke followed Benjamin, his hat in his hands. "What can I'se do, Mr. Ben?"

Benjamin smiled. "I just need to get some food together. There's not much left from what the Freemans gave us, but there should be some things here we can use. The station master tries to keep this cave stocked in case anyone needs to use it. Still, it's been a while since I've come this way, so I'm not sure what's here."

"How come the trackers don' know 'bout this here place?" Dawson asked, throwing another stick onto the fire.

"It's seldom used. Most of the trains move farther east through Ohio," Benjamin told him.

"Then how come you to know about it?"

There was clear suspicion in the older man's voice. Benjamin stopped what he was doing, rising to his full height, which was considerable. His eyes were like polished bronze when he answered.

"I prayed a long time about how God could use me to help my people. And His. I can't say exactly what led me here, but I felt compelled to come this way. By doing so, I met some wonderful Christians who have helped me on my journey. Many times I have come this way when they send me a message to let me know there are others waiting. And like Harriet Tubman, I have never been caught, nor lost a passenger."

Dawson nodded at the gun resting at Benjamin's feet. "I hear that Tubman woman been known to shoot darkies when they hold her up."

Benjamin's face remained serious, although his eyes took on a merry twinkle. "I don't know whether she has or not, but, yes, she has threatened a time or two. When her life and the lives of others are on the line, she does what she thinks is best for everyone."

The vacant look in Dawson's eyes troubled Benjamin when the man's gaze moved from him to the gun. "Would you use that on one of us?"

Knowing it was no idle question, Benjamin looked the man squarely in the eye. "Don't make me find out."

Shrugging, Dawson turned back to the fire. The others glanced uneasily from Benjamin to the rifle lying at his feet. Turning, they each moved away to prepare for the night, one by one, until only Dawson remained.

"These *Christians* of yourn. They be white?"

Benjamin nodded. "They're good people."

Dawson's loud snort was the only answer he received. Frowning, Benjamin shook his head at the other man's obvious dislike of whites. He continued rummaging around through the contents of a crate.

"They're the ones who put the supplies in the millhouse for us. Jacob came to warn us to leave because trackers were in the area."

For the first time Jenny spoke. "They took care of me when I was sick. They gave me food and clothes and even shoes."

Dawson's eyes gleamed as they passed from Benjamin to Jenny and then back again. "My *massa* did the same thing. Then he had me beat when I don' work hard enough."

"The Freemans do what they do because they love the Lord. Several years ago, their grandson was killed by an escaping black slave they were trying to help. The slave stole what little money they had in their house and fled. But the Freemans don't hold that death against *all* blacks. They realize that not all blacks are bad, just as you need to realize that not all whites are bad, Dawson," Benjamin remonstrated softly.

"Well, *I* ain't never seen a good un. You can *keep* yo' white man's God!"

So saying, he turned his back on them, letting them know that his portion of the conversation had ended. Since the man hadn't spoken half a dozen words on the whole trip, Benjamin had been surprised at his loquaciousness now. Exchanging a glance with Jenny, he smiled when she shrugged her shoulders, a rueful grin twisting her lips. He readily changed the subject.

"Since this cave is seldom used, the only food supplies will be things that don't spoil."

With these words, he pulled out a container of hard tack. The hard bread was sealed against the cave's moist interior, but still it crumbled when exposed to the air.

Jenny wrinkled her nose and decided she would rather do without. Instead, she chose to crack some of the shagbark hickory nuts that were piled in the corner. Many of them were covered with mold, but she studiously ignored this and proceeded to open them with a rock. The inside nuts were still edible and quite tasty, Jenny decided, when one was half starving to death.

A packet of dried apples suddenly dropped into her lap, and Jenny jerked her head up in surprise. Benjamin was smiling roguishly down at her.

"We might as well make the most of what we have. These are the last of the supplies the Freemans sent. I was expecting more supplies to be here, but the station master here must not have received word that we would be coming."

Lifting an apple slice, Jenny munched appreciatively as she watched him give bits and portions of food to the others. How easily the man led, and how quickly the others followed. Not surprising, really, when you considered that for the others there had always been someone to give orders. Still, with Benjamin, it was more a matter of absolute trust. Even Dawson allowed Benjamin to lead.

When she glanced Dawson's way, she found the older man watching Benjamin as she had been doing only seconds earlier. There was a feral quality about his gaze that sent a shiver down Jenny's spine. Now *there* was a man she could imagine instigating a riot. She wouldn't trust the man as far as she could throw him, and with his size, that wouldn't be very far.

Hunger somewhat appeased, Jenny lay down on a blanket that had been provided. Everything smelled of dust and decay, but she was too fatigued to be concerned with such things right now. Her body ached in every muscle, but at least the shoes the Freemans had provided her protected her feet from any more bruises and cuts.

Thinking of her shoes brought Amelia and Nathan to mind. Had they escaped? Was someone like Benjamin there for them, to help them make it to freedom? She fervently hoped so. Maybe she would tell Benjamin about them and then he could pray for them. She had more faith in *his* prayers than in her own. Why should God listen to her when she never listened to Him? It didn't occur to her that with such thinking she was admitting a belief in the Almighty.

She was just on the verge of sleep when she was startled awake by a loud moan. Lifting herself on one elbow, she saw Benjamin rise and quickly make his way to where Lila was laying. Bill was softly rubbing her swollen abdomen, his eyes filled with panic. The others barely lifted their heads from their pallets before dropping back to sleep. Only Old Zeke got up and crossed the room.

Jenny pulled herself to a sitting position to better see what was happening. Before long, it became apparent that Lila was in labor. After several tension-filled moments, Benjamin threw Jenny a look across the cavern, which she rightly interpreted as a call for help. Pushing aside the blanket she was huddled under, she quickly made her way to his side.

"What kin I do?" she asked softly.

"Help Lila remain calm. When the baby comes, I'll give it to you." He scrubbed his fingers through his scalp in agitation. "Dear heavens! There's no hope of sanitary conditions here. All I can do is boil a pot of water and at least have clean tools."

Bill studied Benjamin with frantic eyes. "What's that mean?"

Jerked out of his preoccupation, Benjamin smiled reassuringly. "Nothing, Bill. Just that we're going to have to do this the old-fashioned way."

Jenny could tell that Benjamin was worried, but he hid it well. It was important that Bill remain calm so that Lila wouldn't panic. Knowing this, Zeke took his son by the arm and moved him toward the fire.

"Come on, Bill. Let's git outta the way and let Dr. Ben do his job."

Reluctantly, Bill allowed himself to be led away, glancing back frequently over his shoulder. Benjamin turned to Jenny. "Ready?" When she nodded, he asked, "Have you ever helped deliver a baby?"

Again she nodded, dropping down beside Lila and taking

her hand. "Is this your first?" she asked the heaving woman. Before she could answer, Lila gritted her teeth as another spasm of pain shot through her midsection. When the pain subsided, she nodded her head weakly.

"Well," Jenny told her soothingly, "there ain't nothin' to it. Course it's gonna pain somethin' fierce, but that don't last too long. Then you'll have a beautiful baby."

Lila clutched Jenny's hand as Jenny used a rag to rub the perspiration from Lila's forehead. "Don' leave me."

"I won't," Jenny reassured her. She exchanged a look with Benjamin. "How long?"

"Barring unforeseen circumstances, it shouldn't be long. Probably a few hours."

Knowing that for Lila those few hours would seem an eternity, Jenny began to talk to her. Lila concentrated on the questions Jenny asked her, and Benjamin could see the woman's breathing slow. Obviously, Jenny had done this before.

"What you gonna name it?"

"If it's a boy, we want to name him George, after the president," she panted. "If it's a girl, we gonna name her Harriet, after ole Moses."

Suddenly seized with a paroxysm of pain, Lila clenched her eyes tightly, gritting her teeth to keep from screaming out.

"Take deep breaths," Jenny told her, pushing damp black ringlets away from her forehead. She untied the kerchief from around Lila's head and continued smoothing back the curls drenched with perspiration.

Jenny looked around to see if the others were being bothered, but most of them were still asleep. Only Bill and Zeke kept a fireside vigil. Clearly, there was going to be no privacy here in this large cavern. Still, Benjamin moved the lanterns to give them as much privacy as possible without leaving them in darkness.

When the pain passed, Lila lay panting. She clutched the blanket beside her, her eyes wide with anguish and uncertainty. "Is I gonna die, Dr. Ben?"

Benjamin grimaced. He had been asked that question so many times, by so many women. Truth to tell, he was very glad that men didn't have to go through this pain, because frankly he wasn't sure that they could handle it.

"No, Lila," he assured the woman. "It just seems like it. Pretty soon it will all be over."

Eyes full of trust, she dropped her head back against the pallet, content for the moment.

Before long, the pain started in earnest, and both Benjamin and Jenny knew that the time was near. Jenny tried to find a clean cloth to wrap the baby, but there was none.

"By the fire," Benjamin told her.

Jenny found a small piece of blanket hanging beside the fire.

"I washed it when Lila first started her labor. I hoped it would have time to dry before we would need it."

Lifting the cloth from its place, Jenny felt it all over. "It's dry. And warm."

"Good. Leave it there for the time being. When the baby comes, it will still be warm. There's some hot water in the pot and a basin beside the fire with more water. You should be able to give him a bath."

The whole time he had been speaking, Lila had been pushing and grunting. Now with a final scream, the baby came forth, first a tiny head, then tiny hands waving like little flags.

"Correction," Benjamin stated, his voice full of exultation as he quickly tied the umbilical cord. "You can give *her* a bath!"

After the baby received a swat on its backside, the cavern was filled with her piercing cry. No one was asleep now. Without a doubt, Lila's last scream had shaken them from their deep slumber.

Jenny quickly added the hot water to the cold water in the basin until the temperature was finally lukewarm. When she settled the infant in the basin, its crying ceased as the warm water rolled over its body. Jenny smiled, cooing softly to the babe. There was a tender light in her eyes that went unnoticed by all, save one.

Benjamin watched Jenny as she bathed the baby, cleaned her, and then finally wrapped her in the warm blanket. She brought the baby to Lila, now holding her husband's hand and glowing with maternal pride.

Bill stared in awe at the swathed little figure. His grateful eyes meshed with Benjamin's. "Thank you, Dr. Ben! Thank you."

Smiling, Benjamin left them alone. He walked a few paces beyond the light's perimeter and knelt, offering his thanks to God as he always did after a birth. He also prayed for little Harriet, that she might grow to be a woman of God and that she might be raised free.

He felt a presence behind him, and turning, he found Jenny standing slightly off to the side. He could see that she was reluctant to intrude on his private time. Getting quickly to his feet, he motioned her forward. She joined him in the semi-darkness, her eyes shining just as he knew his must be.

"You were wonderful," he told her solemnly.

She shook her head. "No, I didn't do nothin'. I just wanted you to know that I sure was glad you was here."

"I could say the same. I couldn't have done it without you, Jenny. Lila was so frightened."

Jenny's lips tilted into a smile, giving her a saucy look. "*Lila* was frightened? Well, make that *two* of us."

Benjamin laughed. "Well then, that makes *three* of us."

Glancing back at the happy family, Jenny smiled at Zeke cuddling his grandchild. "More like *five* of us."

Benjamin placed an arm around her shoulder as he glanced in the direction she indicated. He couldn't help but smile, but his smile quickly faded. No one had any idea just what a problem this would make for their little group.

Jenny could feel the tenseness of the man beside her as it communicated itself through his nearness. Her own body was not exactly relaxed at his being so close, but hers was a different kind of edginess.

"What's wrong?" she finally asked.

As though coming from far away, his look focused on her face so close to his own. "What?"

"Somethin's botherin' you."

Surprised that she could read him so well, Benjamin dropped his arm and moved to put some distance between them. "Nothing that needs concern you. Let's just have this one moment of beauty and peace."

About to argue, Jenny changed her mind at the resolute look on his face. Shrugging, she turned to leave, but he reached out a hand to detain her.

"Come outside with me?"

Jenny felt a little thrill run through her at the thought of being alone with him. "We needs to sleep," she argued half-heartedly.

Ignoring her statement, Benjamin took her by the hand, and Jenny allowed herself to be led from the cavern. The sun shone brightly against a blue October sky, and it took a moment for their eyes to adjust. It was so dark in the cave, Jenny had forgotten that it was daylight.

For a moment, she allowed the sunlight to bathe her face, reveling in its warmth. It seemed forever since she had been a part of the normal world of daylight and darkness. The plantation seemed so far away, almost as though it were part of another time.

Benjamin stayed close to the mouth of the cave, the shrubbery surrounding the opening hiding them from view. Jenny noticed the direction of his gaze and tried to see what he saw in the distance.

"The river is just beyond those trees."

Surprised, Jenny tried to peer through the dense timberland that separated her from her goal of freedom. The only thing that she could see was what seemed like miles and miles of trees. "Why didn't you say so?"

Sighing, Benjamin dropped to the ground, wrapping his arms around his legs. "I knew Lila would be going into labor, and I also knew that after traveling all night none of us would be in any shape to ford that river."

"Ain't there a boat?"

He shook his head. "No. Not here. If we want to move farther up the river we *might* find a boat, but there's no surety about it. When the trackers find hidden boats, they destroy them."

Jenny dropped down beside him, clutching his arm. "There ain't no boat? Then how we gonna git across?"

Benjamin searched her face, and though she kept her features relaxed, he could see the fear in her eyes.

"We'll swim."

She jumped to her feet, her hands clenching into fists at her side. "I cain't swim! I don' know how!"

He dropped his eyes to the valley below. "I thought as much."

"So what you gonna do?"

"I'll figure that out when we get there."

seven

The sun was just descending below the valley when Jenny went looking for Benjamin. She found him outside the cave's entrance, feet planted apart, hands on hips, face lifted in an attitude of concentration.

"Benjamin."

"Shhh. Listen."

At first Jenny heard nothing but the sighing of the wind through the barren branches of the trees and the periodic call of a bird. Gradually her hearing became more fine tuned, and she could discern the baying of hounds in the distance. Her face paled.

"They've found us!"

Benjamin shook his head. "I don't think so. Sounds more like they're tracking someone else, but it won't be long before the hounds pick up our trail, too."

"What we gonna do?" Jenny's pounding heart belied her calm voice.

Clenching his jaw, Benjamin turned toward the entrance to the cave. "We gotta move."

He strode past Jenny, but she quickly followed him. The tenseness of his face communicated itself to the others and they rose quickly to their feet. All except Lila, who cuddled her nursing baby close, her eyes round with fear.

"What's wrong?" Zeke asked quietly, his face pinched with concern.

"We have to move," Benjamin answered him as he began stuffing items into his pack. The others watched for an instant before they started scrambling to gather their own items together.

"What about Lila and the baby?"

Benjamin's eyes went from Bill standing next to his wife, to Lila still huddled on her pallet, and finally to the now sleeping baby.

"I was hoping to give her a little more time to recover, but I can't. Unless those trackers turn north, they'll be here within six hours."

"I be okay," Lila assured her husband as she took him by the hand. "My mammy had me in the field and kep' on working. I be just as strong."

Kneeling beside Lila, Benjamin told her softly, "Lila, I'm going to have to give the baby something to make her sleep."

Eyes flickering with uncertainty, Lila studied his face. A tentative smile formed on her lips as the trepidation in her eyes was replaced with trust.

"Okay, Dr. Ben."

Benjamin swallowed hard at the look of absolute confidence she bestowed on him. He hated to have to drug the child, but there was really no other way. There could be other trackers in the woods besides the ones he had heard, and the least little sound would alert them to their presence here.

Carefully measuring the paregoric, Benjamin used a dropper to help the baby swallow. It wouldn't take long for the draught to work. He could feel his heart pounding with apprehension. What if he misjudged the dosage? After all, the baby was only hours old. This trip was fast turning into a nightmare. Never before had he faced the problems he was experiencing with this group.

Jenny watched Benjamin, her heart in her mouth. Earlier she had thought about leaving the group if Lila slowed them down. Now, after cradling that tiny body so close, her heart was more involved than she would have believed possible. For the first time since joining the others, she began to think of someone besides herself.

While the others moved about gathering their things, Jenny and Lila watched closely as Benjamin listened to little Harriet's heart and smiled at the reassuring beat.

"So far, so good," he told them, his voice barely above a whisper.

Jenny released her pent-up breath and moved to collect her own belongings. She didn't envy Benjamin his job as leader, and more than ever she found reason to be thankful for his involvement in her own life.

Benjamin hurried them out of the cave, taking a minute to conceal the entrance with surrounding brush. The dusk had yet to turn into full darkness, and Benjamin knew he had to get these people down the hill before it was too dark to see. With trackers so close, there would be no lamplight tonight.

As they traveled, the darkness grew to almost oppressive proportions. In other circumstances, Benjamin would have been glad of the new moon and the darkness it brought to the region, but little Harriet had changed everything. He continually checked to be sure that the infant was still breathing normally. Finally, he had to rely on God's hand in the matter, because his own insecurity was beginning to unsettle Lila and Bill. Forcing himself to stay in the lead, he steered the others quickly toward their destination: the Ohio River.

What seemed an eternity later, but was in reality only four short hours, they exited the woods and found themselves on the river's bank. Benjamin's heart sank. He could hear the wildly rushing river, its waters swollen by the recent rains. Without the light of the moon to guide him, he could not see how swiftly the waters were moving. It would be suicide to attempt the crossing tonight.

He listened closely and could not discern the hounds over the sound of the rushing river. Making a rapid decision, he turned to the others.

"We'll stay here tonight. We'll cross in the morning."

"In the daylight?" Jasper asked incredulously.

"There won't be enough light from the moon for several nights. We have no choice. We can cross before it's fully light, but at least we will be able to judge the water better. If the trackers make it this far, they'll assume no one in their right mind would cross tonight, and if they can't find anyone, they may turn back." He motioned them backward to the forest. "We need to stay hidden. We're too vulnerable in this clearing, so stay among the trees."

While the others hastened to obey, Benjamin began walking up and down the bank collecting small logs. As he dropped a log on the growing stack, Zeke came and stood beside him.

"What you up to, Dr. Ben?"

"I'm hoping to gather enough logs to make a small raft."

"You need some help?" the old man asked, his voice laced with doubt.

It was obvious that the old man doubted Benjamin's judgment. They could hear the wildly rushing river, even if they couldn't see it. Even in the darkness Zeke could see the white of Benjamin's teeth as he flashed the old man a grin.

"I'll take any help I can get."

Benjamin jumped when Jenny's soft voice answered from behind. "Then I'll help, too."

Gathering wood in such inky darkness was a tedious task, but between the three of them they had a nice stack in a very short time. Benjamin sat down next to the logs and pulled some rope from his backpack. There wasn't enough to make a very large raft, but it would have to do.

Using his hands as eyes, Benjamin slowly pieced together a small raft. So intense was his concentration, he failed to hear Jenny approach.

"Benjamin, the baby's awake."

Jumping to his feet, Benjamin felt his way toward where the small ragtag group huddled just inside the first line of trees.

"Lila?"

"Here, Dr. Ben."

He followed the sound of her hissing voice and knelt beside the baby. As his finger stroked the baby's cheek, Harriet's head turned and she latched on to his roving finger with little sucking lips. Grinning, Benjamin told Lila, "She's hungry."

Lila arranged the baby so she could eat undisturbed. "Does you hafta give her mo' sleeping potion, Dr. Ben?"

"I hope not tonight, Lila. But it's important that you don't let her cry. One small, unstifled cry could mean the end of us all."

"I understand. I'll keep her quiet."

"It's cold, Dr. Ben," Annie moaned softly, her teeth chattering. "Cain't we have a fire?"

Before Benjamin could reply, Dawson's harsh voice answered. "Don't be a fool, girl. You such a whiny baby, you gonna git us all kilt."

Although Benjamin could only discern their shadows, he could tell that Annie was huddling close to Jasper.

"You ain't gotta be so mean," the boy snapped at the older man.

"You want me to show you mean, boy?" Dawson snapped back, rising to his feet.

"Enough!" Benjamin told them, stepping between the two, and although his voice was low, it carried a threat of its own. "Settle yourselves down and get some sleep if you can."

He turned to the shivering girl huddled under her one, thin blanket. He felt sorry for her, but there was nothing he could do to alleviate the situation. Taking his own blanket, he wrapped it around Annie. "It's the best I can do, Annie," he told her softly.

"I cain't take yo' blanket, Dr. Ben," she protested, trying to give it back to him. He took the blanket from her hand and wrapped it back around her shivering shoulders.

"Don't argue," he commanded, and she quickly subsided.

Benjamin found a small shelter from the cool wind among a little stand of shrubs. Although he knew he wasn't as cold as Annie, this close to the river he still found himself shivering.

Jenny dropped down next to him. In the darkness he felt her nearness as she wrapped her own blanket around his shoulder and then around her own.

"I thought we kin share," she told him softly.

He was about to argue, but Jenny went on. "I cain't sleep

and I thought maybe you could tell me mo' about the No'th."

Realizing that there would be no sleep for him that night, either, Benjamin conceded. If he talked to Jenny, maybe he could keep the images of rushing rivers and baying hounds from his mind.

He could feel Jenny shivering next to him, and reaching an arm around her waist, he pulled her closer to share his body heat. He suddenly remembered that she was just getting over a bout with pneumonia, and he began to worry what these conditions would do to her.

As the heat from their bodies intertwined among the folds of the blanket, Jenny's shivering began to lessen and then cease altogether. Although her legs were still cold, it was hard to make her mind acknowledge that fact when she was snuggling so close to Benjamin. Her only thoughts were of his nearness and how this might not be such a good idea.

Sensing her agitation, Benjamin began a running monologue, adding bits and pieces to the sketchy account of life in the North that he had previously shared with her. After a time, he could feel her relax.

"It's hard to believe all you say," she murmured skeptically.

"I'm not trying to paint a perfect picture," he disclaimed. "Life in the North is almost as hard on blacks as it is in the South. The difference is, we're free to make our own choices. If a storekeeper dislikes us because of our color, we can go to another. If we want to have a black doctor, we have that choice, too. Still, there is much bigotry in the North from the whites, but there is also much love and compassion."

"How so?"

"Well, it was the white Quakers who started our schools. It was white people who helped us get our communities organized. And it was white people who helped us get the laws changed. After the Revolutionary War, most people in the North believed it was wrong to demand freedom for themselves and then subject others to slavery. At one time, blacks were allowed to vote and hold public office, even in the South."

Benjamin could sense her disbelief by the way she pulled slightly away from him. "It's true," he told her adamantly. "Why even in Georgia blacks weren't denied the vote until 1754."

"You telling me that black people lived in this country just like white folks?"

He nodded and then realized that she couldn't see the movement in the dark. "Yes."

"And you telling me that in the No'th they *still* live that way?"

"Well, except for the voting and holding public offices."

"Benjamin, I cain't even *imagine* it." Her voice was soft with doubt.

For a long time they said nothing, content to listen to the surging waters of the river and think their own thoughts.

Benjamin hoped that one day he would be able to show Jenny the things he had told her, show her that things were just as he said.

As for Jenny, she wondered why she should believe such fantastic stories just because this man sitting next to her should tell her they were so. Her curiosity grew with each bit of information that Benjamin imparted. Curiosity about him, as well as the things and places that he told her about.

Benjamin shifted, turning to face Jenny at the same moment she turned to ask him a question. Their breathing mingled as their lips came within inches. Startled, neither thought to turn away. Truth to tell, neither wanted to.

For a long moment they shared a silent moment of communication before Benjamin slowly lowered his lips and captured Jenny's unerringly in the dark.

His lips fit perfectly against hers, soft and warm, and she allowed herself to revel in his kiss. Never having been kissed before, Jenny opened herself to the joy such an act could bring to two people who cared about one another. Never in her twenty-six years of life had a man touched her in such a way. Always before she had refused to allow herself the joy of knowing a man, knowing that at any moment he might be snatched from her. Her eyes fluttered closed, as did her mind, and nothing existed but the feeling of communion that she wished would never end.

Benjamin pulled back slightly, one hand coming up to cup Jenny's face. He sighed softly. "Jenny." And then his lips claimed hers again and Jenny felt her world rock out of control. Frightened, she pulled away, pushing one hand against his chest where she found his heart racing to match her own.

What was this feeling of wonder she was experiencing? What made her want to hold on to this man and never let him go? Was this then what her sister-in-law had spoken of as *love*? Could it be possible in such a short time?

Sensing that he had frightened her, Benjamin released her.

"I'm sorry," he told her, his voice a husky whisper.

Not sure how to answer, Jenny rose to her feet. Benjamin wrapped one large hand around her wrist to hold her in place, though at the moment her feet couldn't have taken her anywhere. He rose to stand beside her.

"Jenny, I'm sorry."

She was able to see the angles of his face through the darkness and realized that dawn was approaching. What would this day bring? Would she live to see another? Regardless of her fear, she was thankful for being able to experience such a wonderful moment. She lifted a hand to his face, letting her fingers slide down his cheek. "Don't be," she whispered.

Benjamin watched her walk away in the semi-darkness. Dawn would be here quite soon. Realizing that he would be able to see the river now, he moved to the bank and stared somberly into the dark churning water, his thoughts far away.

He was startled out of his reverie when Zeke spoke beside him.

"Might better wait another day or two."

Benjamin shrugged. "I thought the same myself, but we have no food left. Even if we could catch something to eat, we dare not start a fire to cook it. In two days, we would be weak from hunger, and though the river *might* go down, it might not."

The others joined them.

"How many of you can swim?" Benjamin asked. Six pair of terrified eyes stared back at him. Only Dawson seemed unperturbed. His belligerent eyes met Benjamin's.

"I kin swim."

"I kin, too," Jasper told him in a quavery voice. "But that water looks too dangerous fo' me."

Bill studied the rushing water. "I kin swim a little, but I'd never make it in that."

"The rest of you can't swim, not even a little?" Benjamin asked again. The others shook their heads. He moved away to study the water, trying to see the bank on the other side through the dim light. As fast as the water was flowing, it would move them several miles downstream before they reached the other side.

As he stood pondering, a sudden crack split the morning air.

"What was that?" Bill asked fearfully, his eyes searching the forest.

Benjamin's lips pulled down into a frown. "Gunfire. And not too far away."

"Who they shootin' at?" Zeke wanted to know.

"I assume the slaves they were chasing. We've got to go, and go *now*."

Appalled, Jenny pulled away from the group. "You mean back into the forest?"

Benjamin shook his head. "No. I mean across the river."

Jenny stood blinking her eyes as her mind tried to grasp what he had just said. "The river's too fast, and we cants swim. And what 'bout the baby?"

Benjamin was already digging in his sack for the paregoric. "The women and Zeke can sit on the raft and the rest of us men can swim holding on to it. Between the four of us, we should be able to maneuver the raft across the river."

Stepping backwards, Jenny was shaking her head. "That's

crazy. I ain't gonna git kilt for such a fool notion. *I'm* gonna walk upriver."

"How you gonna git across this?" Dawson asked, his voice dripping with sarcasm. "It ain't no better up there."

Benjamin didn't wait for Jenny to make a decision. He began helping Lila tie the now sleeping baby into the material she had used as a carrying sack. Lila snuggled the baby close, her terrified eyes on her husband.

Bill placed a reassuring arm around her shoulders. "Dr. Ben's right. This be our only chance."

Moving the raft to the bank of the river, Benjamin handed Dawson one end of the rope that he had added as a lifeline.

"Help me lower the raft into the river, then hang on to this rope from the bank. I'll hold one side of the raft in the water, you hold the other here. Bill, you help the women get on board. When everyone's on, you and Jasper slide into the water, one on each side. With a man on each corner, we should be able to navigate pretty easily."

Benjamin sounded far more confident than he felt. "Jenny, are you coming?"

There was no way he would leave her behind, but he hoped that she didn't know that. If he had to, he would hog-tie the woman and throw her on the raft himself. She took a moment to decide, her eyes going from the raft, upstream, and back to the raft.

"What if I falls off?" she demanded nervously.

"If you hold on to the rope where it's holding the logs together, you will be okay. But *if* you fall in, I will save you."

She hesitated. What if Benjamin couldn't reach her in time? Had she traveled all this way just to die now? And if she did go upstream, how would she cross there? Wouldn't it be better to take her chances with someone like Benjamin?

His eyes caught and held hers. There was a promise of safety in their dark depths. Another crack of gunfire sounded, much closer this time. Making her decision, Jenny quickly climbed on board. She found a piece of rope and hung on tightly.

"Let's go!"

Benjamin's muscles heaved with the effort of holding the raft in check as the other men slid into the water. Jasper was quickly pulled under, but surfaced clinging to the raft. Spitting water, he nonetheless grinned at them cheerfully.

With its release from the bank, the raft quickly began gliding downstream. The four men kicked with all their might, trying to guide it across to the other side.

The cold water numbed Benjamin's limbs and he had to concentrate to keep himself moving. Glancing over his shoulder, he could see the others having the same problem. Too long in this water would not be healthy for any of them.

The women lay on the tiny structure, their hands clinging to rope holds. It was from vigilant old Zeke that they had their first warning of trouble.

"Look out!"

It took several seconds for Benjamin to see what the semi-darkness had hidden from him. Cursing himself for a fool, Benjamin saw too late the debris-littered waters. If only he had waited until it was lighter, but now it was too late.

Rubble from the twisters flooded the water in dangerous zigzagging patterns. There was nothing they could do now but try to dodge the litter and make it to the other side.

Moving in unison, the four men tried to dodge their way past the skimming logs. Benjamin heard Jenny's scream in time to lift his head from the water and see a dead cow float past their raft. Gritting his teeth, he pressed on.

Glancing back over his shoulder, Benjamin saw Zeke trying to dislodge tree limbs that were knocking against the side of their raft. He offered up a prayer for the old man's safety, praying that he wouldn't lose his balance.

They were almost to the other side when Benjamin noticed a large tree headed straight for them. "Swim harder!" he yelled, his voice almost drowned by the rushing waters.

The other men noticed the tree bearing down upon them and started kicking with all their might. Benjamin thought that they had made it, but as the tree passed them, it rolled in the water and a jutting branch caught the edge of the raft. The raft was knocked to the side, and Benjamin watched helplessly as Zeke was catapulted over the side and into the churning river. Since he was at the lead of the raft, he knew he couldn't let go or the raft would be sent spinning.

The old man surfaced twenty feet away, clawing the water as he gasped for air. As Benjamin watched, another head surfaced next to Zeke. Dawson!

Benjamin kept moving forward until the raft bumped the shore. Between Bill, Jasper, and himself, they were able to get it secured.

Turning back to the river, Benjamin searched for the other two men. They were nowhere in sight. Bill began running downstream, screaming as he ran. "Papa! Papa!"

Benjamin dropped to his knees, his chest heaving with the exertion of breathing. He heard Jenny's gasp. Noticing the direction of her gaze, he glanced across the river. There on the other side was a mounted posse of armed white men.

eight

For an instant Benjamin froze, his mind rapidly trying to adjust to the situation. Forcing his body to answer his summons, he climbed wearily to his feet.

"We gots to get outta here!"

For a minute Jenny's words didn't register. Lila stepped forward angrily.

"We cain't leave Bill. And what 'bout Zeke and Dawson?"

Slowly the strength was returning to Benjamin's limbs. He could see the trackers on the other side of the river as they searched up and down the banks for a safe way to cross. Thankfully, the debris-choked river made even the hardiest reluctant to enter the water. Benjamin realized that if the morning had been any more advanced, he probably would not have crossed either and they would now be in the hands of those men across the river.

It bought them a little time, but not much. The men would merely go farther upriver and use a larger raft or one of the barges. And on horseback, they could return to this spot in far less time than his party would need to put some distance between them.

"We have to go," he concluded, reluctant to commit to such an action. If only there were some way he could leave the others safely and return to search for the missing men. If they hadn't been spotted, he could have chanced it. But not now.

Lila refused to budge. She bundled Harriet against her shoulder and vehemently shook her head when Benjamin tried to reason with her.

"Lila," he told her calmly, "I'll try to come back for them, but right now I have to get you all to safety. If those trackers catch you, you may never see Bill again." His eyes went briefly to the sleeping child. "Or little Harriet, for that matter. Do you want to lose your baby *and* your husband?"

Her shoulders sagged with defeat. He saw such pain in the dark brown eyes Lila lifted to his face that he almost relented. But losing everyone to those men wouldn't help *anyone*.

Jasper quietly lifted Bill's pack to his own shoulders and fell into step behind the women as Benjamin headed their group out.

Jenny walked just behind Benjamin, her mind trying to close out the picture of old Zeke as he catapulted off of the raft. All she could think of was the pain she would feel if that had been her own pappy. She had grown fond of the old man and even now her heart felt heavy at the thought that he might be dead.

"Where we goin'?" she finally asked the taut figure in front of her.

"There's another station a few miles from here."

"But won't those trackers come lookin' fo' us there?" Jasper asked fearfully.

"Probably, but there's an underground tunnel that is well hidden. Even if they stop at this house, they won't find you."

It took Jenny a moment to realize that Benjamin had said *you* and not *us*. She wondered if it was a mere slip of the tongue or if Benjamin planned on leaving them at this station. Almost as if he could read her mind, he answered her unasked question.

"I'll leave you there. It won't be safe to move for a few days, and the man who lives there will give you food and shelter."

Appalled, Jenny pulled him to a stop. "Where you goin'?"

His look rested on her briefly before going to each of the others. "You'll be safe there for a few days. I'm going back to see if I can find the others."

Lila looked relieved, Jasper and Annie uncertain. Jenny was stunned.

"Who gonna git us from here to Canada if somethin' happens to you?"

Right now she could care less about Canada. Her only

thought was for the safety of this big ox who at times didn't seem to have the sense God had given to a Catawba worm. Jenny was angry and growing angrier by the minute.

"You're in Illinois now," he told her patiently. "This is a free state. If not for those men at the river, we could travel more openly, but all they have to do is catch us and claim that we belong to them. *None* of us would be allowed to argue the case in court."

"But you free," Annie told him, clearly puzzled. "They cain't do nothin' to you!"

Benjamin sighed. "The law says different. But that's beside the point. I have no intention of getting caught, only I move faster when I'm alone."

Turning, he began to stride forward again, the others uncertainly dropping into step behind him. There was no path here, and Jenny wondered how Benjamin could possibly know where they were going. The brush and trees tore at her skin until she thought there must not be a place on her body that didn't have some kind of bruise, sore, or cut.

Turning her mind to last night's encounter helped divert her mind from her troubles, but it increased her ire with the man striding along so confidently ahead of her. She was beginning to care for Benjamin, and she knew that was what irritated her most. She didn't want to care for him. Never before had she allowed a man to touch her feelings, and to do so now, with Benjamin, was only courting disaster. The difference in their lifestyles was only a small part of it. Loving Benjamin would enslave her in a different kind of way and could only lead to heartache, and she didn't want that for her life.

That brought to mind another question. What exactly *did* she want to do with her life? Until now she hadn't really given it much thought. Her only desire had been for freedom, but she was rapidly learning that with freedom came responsibility. For the first time in her life, she had to learn to make wise decisions.

Before long they came to a clearing where a small log cabin

nestled among the trees. Benjamin halted the group before carefully maneuvering until he could see the structure from all sides. His searching gaze found what he was looking for, and with a relieved sigh, he told the others to follow him.

When he knocked on the door, they could hear shuffling of feet before a voice inquired, "Who's there?"

"A friend with friends," Benjamin answered quietly.

The door opened a crack before being thrust wide and a grinning old Negro stood before them. His smile lit up his face as he pumped Benjamin's hand up and down.

"Benjamin! Mighty good to see you!" He turned his look on the others. "And these be friends of yourn?"

Benjamin nodded. "We need shelter, Thomas, and something to eat. But first, you better take down your quilt. There are trackers bound to be here within hours."

Thomas didn't wait to ask questions but hurried outside, returning with the quilt bundled into his arms. The quilt would be returned to the line only when the danger to runaways was past. This had been the symbol agreed upon by stations in this part of the country to alert runaways of a safe house, and all the conductors who traveled this area recognized it.

"Git on down to the tunnel," Thomas commanded sharply. "I'll cover things behind you."

Benjamin crossed the room, and as he moved aside a cabinet next to the fireplace, a small opening appeared. Thomas handed him a candle.

"Careful now," Thomas admonished as Benjamin helped each one descend the wooden ladder.

After everyone was in the tunnel, Thomas hurried to gather some food. He handed it to Benjamin and the two men exchanged looks.

"Be careful, Thomas. They'll be coming here, I know it."

Snorting softly, Thomas grinned. "Don' you worry none about me. You just keep them folks quiet till them scalawags is gone."

"I won't be staying long. I have to go back and see if I can find three other men who met with an accident."

Thomas studied the younger man gravely. "That's not a wise idea, my friend. There's been a lot of activity in these woods since them twisters hit down south."

"I know. But I have to go. It's *you* I'm concerned about. What if they decide to take you south?"

"Now what they want with an old man like me, huh?" Thomas scoffed. "I be okay. I ain't never been bothered befo'. I'm way too old for them slavers to think they can git any money outta this old hide."

Benjamin was unconvinced. True, Thomas had lived here as a free man for some twenty years now, but there was always the chance someone would take it in his head to be unscrupulous enough to try and make a few dollars by selling the old man down south. There was no one here to know, Thomas's wife having died some years ago, leaving him entirely alone.

"Still," Benjamin cautioned, "be careful."

Nodding, the old man moved the cabinet back into place, plunging the group into darkness relieved by the light of only one small candle.

Benjamin set the candle on a small sill dug into the walls of the dirt tunnel. The darkness here was almost as intense as the cave, only in the cave there had been lantern light to alleviate the darkness. Here there was only one small candle.

"Cain't you light the lantern?" Annie asked.

"No, and you mustn't talk," Benjamin told her in a fierce whisper. "Although we can't hear what is happening above us, it's quite possible that someone might hear us. You mustn't speak at all, not unless you go farther into the tunnel. But remember, sound carries."

That was all the censure Annie needed. She retreated into fearful silence, the others doing the same.

Time seemed to tick by ever so slowly. The utter silence, the absolute stillness frightened Jenny more than anything had to this point. Surrounded by darkness, with no sound save their breathing, it was almost as though they had been thrown into some dark void. Were it not so cold, Jenny would have compared it to the stories of Hell that her mother had regaled her with as a child.

Mama had told her that Hell, real Hell, was eternal separation from God. In Hell there would be no light, because God is the source of all light, and without Him there would be total darkness.

Annie started whimpering and Jasper slid down next to her. Wrapping an arm around the terrified girl, he pulled her close. She snuggled into his embrace, the sounds of her weeping ceasing, but the tears falling in an ever-increasing torrent.

Benjamin handed them each several sandwiches made of biscuits and ham. They devoured the tasty meal, finally ending their fast of the last several hours.

Taking a dipper of water from a bucket in the corner, Benjamin handed it first to Lila and then the others, ending with Jenny.

She wrinkled her nose at the musty taste of stale water, but as thirsty as she was, she still wanted more. Benjamin handed her another dipperful when she nodded her head at the bucket. Thirst finally slaked, Jenny leaned back against the dirt wall.

Benjamin settled next to her, close, but not touching. Still, Jenny was acutely aware of every little move he made. When his eyes met hers, even in the dark she could read their message. There was something powerful that seemed to flash between them. It amazed her that the others were unaware of it. Each moment spent in his company seemed to increase the awareness between them.

The moment was broken by a small sound coming from the corner of the little room. A small animal streaked across the lighted space, whiskers twitching, small round ears alert for movement.

Jenny rose to her feet, a scream lodged in her throat. Before it could find release, Benjamin was beside her shoving a heavy palm across her mouth.

"Don't scream," he whispered vehemently.

One look from those intense eyes, and the scream died in her throat. Shuddering, she nodded her head to let him know that she understood. Slowly he released the pressure on her mouth, his hand sliding down her throat and dropping to his side. She quickly stepped away from him, wrapping her arms tightly around her midsection as she tried not to cry.

When Jenny glanced at the others, she found Lila with her head buried in the folds of the baby's blanket and Annie hid against Jasper's chest. Both had apparently seen the rat as well. Not willing to chance close proximity with the rodent again, Jenny remained standing.

Taking her by the shoulders, Benjamin pulled her closer to the candle so that she could read his face. Bending, he whispered softly in her ear, "I'm sorry I frightened you."

His breath fanned against her ear, sending a shiver of awareness throughout her body. Dropping her eyes, she nodded to let him know that she accepted his apology. When he moved away, the lost warmth from his hands left her colder than before.

Time edged slowly forward until Jenny thought she would scream. How long had it been since they had come into this dark hole? And how much longer would they have to stay?

They all jumped when they heard the cabinet being moved from above. Benjamin motioned them farther into the darkness as he blew out the candle. They released a collective sigh of relief when Thomas's grinning face came into view.

"They done come and gone," he told them softly. "But I think they pretty sure you're here somewhere. Or at least that you will be. I saw a man slip into the woods on the other side of the clearing. They's watching the house."

"Did they search the house?" Benjamin asked as he relit the candle.

"Yep. Thought they was gonna find the tunnel for sure, but they didn't."

Benjamin silently offered thanks to God for their protection. "Have the others gone on then?"

"Yep. Just the one over in the woods left."

"How soon till it's dark?"

" 'Bout three hours, I'd say." Thomas lifted a bucket from the floor beside him. "Sorry 'bout the water. Weren't expecting no company."

Benjamin took the bucket from him, handing him the bucket of stale water in its place.

"I'll fix some stew for later."

"Thanks," Benjamin replied wearily. The hours without sleep were beginning to tell on him.

Thomas handed down extra quilts. "I knows it be cold down there, but it be safer than up here in case they come back."

"I know. Thanks for everything."

Benjamin distributed the blankets to the others, saving one for himself. Thomas waited until they were settled before closing the hole in the wall.

"We'd best get some sleep," Benjamin told them, his voice drained of emotion. He went to Lila, kneeling to examine the baby. The paregoric was wearing off. He knew he had to let the child eat, but then he would have to drug her again. This tenseness over the baby was going to cause him to make some serious mistakes if he wasn't careful.

Deciding to take a chance on the paregoric having a residual effect on the baby, Benjamin allowed her to feed and go back to sleep on her own. Hopefully, the effects of the paregoric would last a few more hours and he could get some sleep without worry.

He settled himself on his blanket, mindless of the damp and cold. Almost instantly, he was asleep.

❧

Jenny watched Benjamin sleeping, an oddly protective feeling running over her. Relaxed in slumber, his face bore no traces of anxiety.

She allowed her eyes to roam over his features, wishing she could let her fingers follow in their wake. High cheekbones spoke of Indian ancestry. He had told her that the first blacks in this country intermingled with the Indians, even fighting against whites. That had been long before the Revolutionary War.

What would it be like to "jump the broom" with a man such as he? Strong and passionate, gentle yet decisive, her married life would be anything but dull. Still, being married to a man like Benjamin would mean submitting herself to another kind of servitude, because he would always be the master in his own home. Idly, she wondered if he had Ashanti blood in his veins as well.

Pulling her quilt closer, she snuggled down into its folds, and before long her dreamy reflections were interrupted by a deep sleep.

❧

Benjamin was pulled from a profound slumber by the opening of the hole at the top of the ladder. Instantly he was on his feet, all traces of sleep swept away as fear sent his blood surging through his veins. He reached for the rifle that was never far from his side.

"Benjamin?"

The hoarse whisper stirred a sense of panic in the others. Everyone was promptly on their feet.

"Thomas! What is it?"

"It's dark. The man still be across the road, though. Maybe you should wait."

Benjamin began gathering the items he would need. "I can't. I have to know, one way or another. If they're out there, they will need help finding shelter."

"God be wit you, then," the old man told him earnestly.

Thomas pushed the cabinet back against the wall once more, enclosing them in gloom. Benjamin lifted his pack, throwing it across his shoulders. As Jenny watched his retreating form disappear down the tunnel, she suddenly felt as though she were losing something precious. An eerie premonition of impending doom sent her scurrying after him.

"Benjamin, wait."

Her whispered words made him pause. Turning back to her,

he waited until she caught up with him. "What is it?"

She laid an urgent hand against his forearm. "Please don't go!"

Although it was too dark to see his face, she could hear the frown in his voice. "What? Why?"

How could she begin to explain when she didn't understand these feelings herself?

"I have to hurry," he told her impatiently. His hand found her cheek, and he rubbed his thumb slowly across her lips. "I'll be all right. Just stay put here until I return."

"But what if you don't?"

"I will. Pray for me."

Benjamin could feel Jenny tense in the darkness. Although she claimed not to believe in God, he knew that wasn't so. Something held her away from the love God so wanted to give her, and Benjamin was very much afraid that it was her own pride.

"But what if you don't?" she insisted. "What the rest of us gonna do?"

"Thomas knows what to do. Trust him."

"Let me come with you."

Benjamin's other hand came up to cup her other cheek. He pulled her face closer to his own. "I can't. You'll be safe here. Please, Jenny. Obey me."

Jenny wanted to argue. Always before obedience had been demanded of her, and sometimes she gave in willingly, sometimes not. Never had anyone pleaded for her obedience.

"All right," she finally conceded softly. "I'll stay."

He lifted her face for a kiss before quickly releasing her and feeling his way to the end of the tunnel. Once there, he pushed at the ceiling and an opening appeared.

Jenny could tell when Benjamin was gone from the tunnel. When he was near, the very air seemed alive with his presence. Now she was left in cold darkness again with only her own fearful thoughts and reflections to keep her company.

Shivering, she moved back to the others.

❧

Benjamin skirted the sentry in front of Thomas's house, easily evading detection. He moved cautiously through the woods back in the direction of the river. Each crackle of the underbrush caused his heart to thunder in panic. If he was to be caught. . .well, it didn't bear thinking about.

It took some time for him to backtrack to the river and then to find the exact spot where they had landed their raft. Barely any light came from a sliver of moon, but he found the raft torn apart, most of the logs sent downriver with the other debris.

The chill air from off the river raised the flesh on his arms. He made his way farther downstream, hoping to find where the others had left the water. Instead, he found horse prints. A divided set. The group had split, some going in the direction of Thomas's cabin, the others going downriver.

He prayed fervently as he ran along. Each step took him farther away from Jenny and the others; but he went on, knowing he could never rest until he knew what had happened to the other men. He had never lost a passenger before, and he didn't want to start now.

The night was waning and still he had found no sign of the others nor their hunters. He stopped. He had no clear plan in mind, and rushing into a situation without one was pure foolishness. Although he had never stopped praying, he strengthened his petitions now. He didn't know what else to do.

He sat on a log trying to think where he should go from here. It would take him several hours to get back to the others, and there weren't many hours of darkness left.

The last thing he remembered was a sound behind him.

❧

For two days Jenny sat in the dark tunnel almost beside herself with worry. Benjamin hadn't returned and her distress was growing with each passing moment. He had told her he would return. He had also told her to trust Thomas. Well, Thomas she trusted, but Benjamin still hadn't come.

Now, little Harriet was growing restless and irritable. It

took all of Lila's time trying to keep the infant from crying, and no one else dared to administer the sleeping drug.

Maybe she was selfish, but Jenny didn't want to be caught and taken back to captivity. From everything Benjamin had told her, she could never be sure whether she would be sent to her own home plantation. She could be sold to someone else, and her family would never know.

Even Jasper was growing restless, yet his patience with Annie seemed to be unending. Jenny watched them conversing quietly together. They seemed to have forgotten Benjamin's admonition to remain silent. Irritated, Jenny moved toward the end of the tunnel where Benjamin had disappeared.

Lately, she had been giving serious consideration to leaving on her own. Thomas could help the others, but she could always find her way with the drinking gourd. Even Benjamin relied on those stars to lead the way, although at times he seemed to know the paths through the woods just as well without them.

Time seemed to cease in the tunnel. They didn't know whether it was day or night. The only inclination they had of the passage of time was when Thomas would open the door to give them food or check on their wants.

A small hole had been dug to be used for nature's call. Each time they filled in more of the hole with dirt, but the stench was beginning to grow. Thomas told them that no one had ever had to stay so long before.

This was hardly reassuring to Jenny. She couldn't shake the feeling that something dreadful had happened to Benjamin.

They could hear Thomas moving the cabinet. Jenny stood at the bottom of the ladder staring upward at the sudden brilliance. Shielding her eyes with her hands, she blinked rapidly to focus against the burning light.

Thomas's worried face came into view. "I think something's wrong," he told them. "The guard across the road has left."

"Mebbe they gots tired of waitin'," Jasper suggested as he moved next to Jenny.

"Mebbe," Thomas agreed, but he didn't sound too reassuring.

"What we gonna do?" Lila asked. It was the first time she had spoken in two days, except when she was cuddling Harriet.

"You'll come on up here now. That tunnel ain't no fittin' place for a youngun. It should be safe enough. We'll keep watch."

Jasper climbed the ladder first, helping the others up behind him. Thomas motioned to the pot of hot water on the stove. "You kin bathe the baby if you want. All you kin bathe. I gots plenty of water from the spring."

Thankfully, Jenny took her turn with the others as each one washed first their body, then their clothes. Thomas provided blankets to wrap around them until their clothing could dry.

It took some time for everyone to get themselves into some kind of order before Thomas called them all to the table. For a man, Thomas was an extremely accomplished cook. Jenny supposed living alone, he had to make do.

As tasty as the food was, Jenny picked at the stew, her appetite gone. What were they supposed to do now? Were they supposed to wait longer for Benjamin's return?

A sudden knock at the door had everyone scurrying for the tunnel. Everyone except Jenny. Something held her still as Thomas made his way to the door.

"Who's there?" he asked roughly.

"A friend, wit a friend."

The voice was too muffled to distinguish, but Jenny was sure it wasn't Benjamin. Thomas glanced over his shoulder, motioning Jenny into the tunnel. She did as she was bid, but still kept the opening partially disclosed.

Thomas carefully opened the door, shielding the room from view. Suddenly he was shoved backwards, stumbling as two men fell into the room. One man was carrying another and both were covered in blood. As the one man dropped the other to the floor, he had to stagger to keep himself upright.

The breath rushed out of Jenny, her eyes widening in alarm. She was across the room in an instant, kneeling beside the man on the floor.

"Benjamin!"

nine

Two days earlier, when Benjamin had opened his eyes, a shadowy form was standing over him in the murky darkness. Disoriented, he lay still, trying to reason out his situation. Before he could make any kind of move, a large man knelt by his side.

"You okay?"

In the tenebrous gloom it was impossible to distinguish features, but Benjamin realized that the voice was not a white one.

When he tried to sit up, the world spun about him in a kaleidoscope of colors. Moaning, he lay back to the cold ground. "What happened?"

"I'se really sorry. I thought you was a paddy roller." The man's voice was truly repentant.

Everything was beginning to come back to him now. The other man helped him sit up and Benjamin waited until the waves of dizziness passed. For the first time, he realized that the man wasn't alone. He peered through the dim light, trying to discern the identity of the other person. He could barely make out the shadowy outline of a woman.

"Are you runaways?"

The big man lifted himself to his feet, but refused to answer. Benjamin could feel the tension rising from the couple, but he was unsure of the reason.

"I can help you find a safe house not far from here," he told them, trying to relieve them of their fear. Suspicions were rising on both sides.

"You don' sound like no darkie," the man told Benjamin skeptically.

Benjamin climbed unsteadily to his feet. Often he found himself to be the object of a passenger's distrust because of his education. At times, it could be a decided handicap.

"I'm from Pennsylvania. Do you know where that is?"

"In the No'th."

Benjamin grinned wryly. To most plantation slaves, people were either from the North or the South. He wondered what they would think if they knew just how different the attitudes in various states, regardless of region, could be.

"I'm a conductor," he tried to reassure the couple. "I'm taking some others to safety and if you would like, you are welcome to come along."

The man hesitated a moment before he finally said, "I'se looking fo' a man. Some folks told us he could hep us and that he lived here somewheres."

"That would be Thomas," Benjamin answered him. "You came from another station?" Had they perhaps been sent here by the Freemans?

The other man answered his question with one of his own. "How come you be out here alone if you wit others?"

"We had an accident this morning." Had it only been this morning? It seemed a lifetime away. "I was trying to find three black men who became separated from our party."

The only sound that could be heard was the loud chirruping of crickets and croaking of frogs in the woods around them. A chill breeze sent a shiver skittering down Benjamin's spine. He wondered why the other man had suddenly become so still.

"Did you say three men?"

"Yes." Benjamin's heart began to hammer furiously in his chest. Something in the man's voice warned him that something was seriously wrong. "Have you seen them?"

"I don' rightly knows. We saw *one* man."

The woman drew close against the man's side and he placed a protective arm around her waist. Benjamin could hear her choked sob and wondered at its cause.

"Where did you see him? What did he look like?"

Again there was that pause before the other man answered him, and when he did, his voice was rough with emotion. "He were hanging from a tree."

Legs suddenly weak, Benjamin sank slowly to the ground. It wasn't possible. It *had* to be someone else. But even so. . .

"I buried him," the big man told Benjamin softly.

The throbbing ache in Benjamin's head was nothing compared to the one in his heart. How could people be so cruel to each other? And what had the man done that was so deserving of death? And for that matter, was it Zeke, Bill, or Dawson? He had to find out.

Getting to his feet, Benjamin asked the other man, "Where did you bury him?"

Even in the darkness, Benjamin could see the whites of the other man's eyes as they widened in surprise.

"What you gonna do, mister?"

"I have to find out if it was one of my group. I have to know."

"I think you crazy, but I shows you where it's at."

Placing a detaining hand on his arm, Benjamin told him, "No. Just tell me. I'll go on my own. You take your woman and go to the station I was telling you about. I'll tell you how to get there. It's not safe in these woods right now."

"But you gonna stay?" The man clearly doubted his sanity.

"I have to."

Benjamin told them how to get to Thomas's cabin. As they started to walk away, Benjamin asked, "What are your names?"

The man paused before answering. It was clear he was still suspicious of Benjamin's presence in these woods.

"My name be Simon. This here be my wife, Sarah."

Benjamin nodded, though they couldn't see him in the dark. "Well, Simon, tell Thomas that Benjamin sent you."

Turning, he made his way toward the area where Simon had buried the body. With each step, he petitioned the Lord that he wouldn't find one of his party beneath that cold mound. He hadn't gone far before he located a hill of dirt among all the fallen leaves.

His prayer was answered in the negative. He stared solemnly

down on Dawson's still form, dirt still clinging to his twisted features. Benjamin's fingers stroked gently across the rope burns on the dead man's neck before he rose quickly to his feet and recovered the body in its shallow grave. Bowing his head, he prayed silently.

There was no time for mourning. Now he had to find Zeke and Bill. But how? And where to begin?

As he lifted his head from his prayer, Benjamin noticed horse tracks and among them footprints. Hurrying over, he studied the ground before determining that the group was heading back south. They must have decided to forego searching for the others in his party for some odd reason. Something wasn't right here, but he couldn't figure out what it was. His head told him to wait and think this through, but his burdened heart made him hurry through the night without thought to consequences.

He followed the trail and before long came upon a group of white men resting around a fire, their rifles close to their sides. Searching the area with a swift glance, Benjamin spotted Bill and Zeke tied to a large tree at the far end of a clearing. His heart leaped at the sight of them, alive, if not particularly well.

The men around the fire were somewhat relaxed, but would tense at the least sound. They seemed to be expecting someone, and whatever it was they were anticipating didn't seem to make them too happy.

Both Bill and Zeke were tied standing, and Zeke's form hung limply against the ropes that bound him. The old man was clearly ill. Bill's eyes were fastened upon the apparent leader of the group. As the flames from the fire reflected in them, Benjamin could read no fear in their cold, dark depths. The look Bill was giving the other man was filled with an angry hatred.

Benjamin was trying to decide what to do when the air was split with rifle fire and one of the trackers slumped to the ground. For a moment, everyone seemed frozen in time. In the next instant, there was sudden pandemonium.

It didn't take Benjamin but a moment to realize what was happening. These attackers were obviously vigilantes, white abolitionists who were constantly on the lookout for trackers taking slaves back to their life of slavery. They were prevalent in his home in Philadelphia as well, which was one reason that Benjamin had very little fear of someone trying to claim him as a slave.

The trackers had scattered, the vigilantes close on their heels. Guns were being fired indiscriminately, shells ricocheting from the nearby trees. Benjamin saw a shell splinter the tree near Bill's head. Forgetting his own safety, he plunged across the forest trying to reach the clearing. A fiery pain sliced through his shoulder as he entered a thicket of brush, knocking him to the ground.

❧

So intense was her concentration on Benjamin's unconscious form that Jenny failed to give much notice to the man standing beside him.

"Jenny!"

Startled, Jenny lifted her eyes from Benjamin's prostrate body to the man towering next to her. She rose quickly to her feet.

"Nathan!"

Thomas came and knelt beside Benjamin, his hands moving to find any injuries. "You two knows each other?"

Jenny barely heard the old man. "Where's Amelia?"

Nathan looked from Thomas back to her. She could see the uncertainty in his eyes.

"It's okay, Nate. Thomas is a friend."

Relief quickly flooded Nathan's features and his shoulders relaxed. "Then I made it!"

Confused, Jenny was about to ask questions when she heard a moan at her feet. She dropped to the floor, ashamed that she had forgotten Benjamin for the moment. She looked at Thomas.

"Will he be okay?"

The old man's lips turned down into a frown. His eyes sliced upward glaring at Nathan. "What happened, boy? This be a gunshot wound."

Jenny sucked in a quick breath. "Shot!"

While Thomas crossed to the fire to retrieve hot water, Jenny began to unbutton Benjamin's shirt. A gaping wound was exposed on his left shoulder, and as her fingers gently probed the injury, Benjamin moaned, moving his head from side to side.

Nathan stood silently watching the two as they ministered to the injured man. Jenny decided that questions could wait. Her main concern right now was for Benjamin. One question refused to be dislodged from her mind, however, and once again she questioned Nathan.

"Amelia?"

For a minute he didn't answer.

"Nate! Where's Melia?"

"She be safe," was all he would tell her.

Thomas glanced up at the big man suspiciously. There was something the big darkie was not telling them. "Help me git him onto the bed."

Together the men gently lifted Benjamin and placed him on Thomas's bed. Jenny settled the covers over Benjamin's lower body but left his upper torso free for Thomas to work on. Benjamin's brows creased into a frown and he moaned again, but he remained unconscious.

"How bad is it, Uncle Thomas?"

The old man patted Jenny's hand absently. "It's a bad wound, but it be clean. The bullet went clean through." He glanced at Nathan again. "They's a knot the size of a plum on the back of his head, though. I'll ask you again. What happened?"

"What happened to Benjamin?"

Three pair of eyes turned simultaneously to the opening beside the fire. Jasper was at the top of the ladder, his body hidden from view. Nathan's eyes went wide as the young boy climbed into the room.

"That's what we trying to find out," Thomas told him in aggravation.

One by one the others climbed the ladder into the room. Nathan watched them, his face a study in amazement.

"You be the railroad man?" Nathan inquired, never taking his eyes from the people surrounding him.

"Boy! What's the matter with you? You tetched in the head or somethin'? Course I am. Why else you here?"

When Nathan looked back at the old man, his eyes were serious. "I had to be sure."

Jenny lightly placed a hand on his arm. "It's okay, Nate. This be a safe place." She nodded her head at Benjamin. "He be a conductor on the Railroad. Thomas here be one of the stations. You understand?"

Although he had no reason to trust the others, Nate knew Jenny. His shoulders relaxed as he nodded his head in confirmation.

"So tell us what happened," Thomas growled.

As Nathan related his story, Thomas worked to clean Benjamin's wound.

"I didn't knows he was a darkie. It were too black out to see clear. When I saw him sittin' there, all I could think was that he were between me and safety." His look fastened on Jenny. "I didn't try to kill him, Jenny, honest."

Jenny wanted more than anything to sit next to Benjamin on the bed and will him into consciousness, but she was afraid of what the others might think of such an action. Besides, there was nothing she could do that Thomas couldn't do equally well.

"It's okay, Nate. Just tell us how he gots shot. You didn't have no gun."

"But Benjamin did," Jasper interrupted, his eyes full of suspicion as they focused on Nathan.

Nathan glared back at him. "I didn't do it. It was the paddy rollers."

Just the name struck fear into all their hearts. Thomas came quickly to his feet. "Paddy rollers? They must be close. You better gits back in the tunnel."

Nathan shook his head. "They close, but they not gonna hurt no one no mo'."

Now Jenny was growing irritated. "You not making sense, Nate."

"They's dead."

The room grew so silent that it was possible to hear the wind whistling outside the cabin.

"You better start at the beginning," Thomas instructed quietly, never taking his eyes from Benjamin.

So Nathan told them all that had transpired in the last two days.

"After he sent me on my way, he went to find the others. I heard lots of shootin', but I wasn't there to see what happened."

Jenny interrupted, clutching the big man's arm. "Nate, where's Amelia?"

Nathan studied the group around him before going and opening the door. He sent a sharp, piercing whistle out across the darkness. Before long, they could hear shuffling at the door.

Jenny held her breath, releasing it with a sharp cry as she ran across the room to enfold her friend in a hug.

Amelia hugged Jenny back, her face full of wonder. "Jenny! Jenny, is it really you?"

"Oh, Melia! I thought I'd never see you again!"

Both girls continued laughing, hugging, and crying as Nathan closed the door behind them. Thomas cleared his throat.

"If you don't mind, I still wants to know how Benjamin gots this here gunshot wound."

Her mind brought sharply back to the present, Jenny moved back to Benjamin's side. His face was paler than usual and sweat was beading across his brow.

"Yes, Nate. How did this happen?"

"Well, like I says, I wasn't there to see it. I heard all the gunshots and I was scared. I started to runs with Melia, but somethin' made me stop. Somethin' tolds me to go check things out."

Something, he said. Could that something have been Benjamin's God? The God who seemed to watch over him so carefully. But if that was the case, why was he lying here now with the uncertainty of death looming in the distance?

"When I gots to the place, I found several dead men. They just laying there with no one else abouts. When I turned to runs, I fell over this here man. He were lying in the bushes."

Forgetful of the others in the room, Jenny sat next to Benjamin on the bed, her eyes filled with tenderness as she watched his chest rise and fall. *Poor Benjamin*, she thought as she stroked gentle fingers across his forehead. He would die to save others even though he barely knew them. Jesus had done the same, and for the first time that she could remember, she felt shame for her rejection of Him.

Benjamin was as much a slave as she, even though he was legally a free man. The difference was, he *chose* to be a slave. He loved his Master and served Him with devotion. If she really thought about it, her parents were much the same way. Although they were owned legally by the Jacksons, they served with love and loyalty. They were content to be servants, knowing that they were loved in return.

Jenny's problem was that she just didn't want to submit to *anyone*. Was this why she rejected the God her mother had taught her about? Was she afraid that it would make her a slave all over again?

"He been in and out of it ever since," Nathan continued. "That's why it took us so long to find this place. I think he gots a fever, 'cause he kept telling us 'bout someone named Jacob. That's why I wasn't sure it be you," he told Thomas.

The old man grunted, busy with his task. He took a long bladed knife and lay it in the fire. Jenny questioned him with her eyes.

"I gots to seal that wound. It keep bustin' open. But that's probably why it ain't infected yet."

Jenny swallowed hard, her stomach churning at the thought of the pain about to be administered. Even though Benjamin was still unconscious, Thomas had the men hold him firmly to the mattress.

Swiftly and efficiently, Thomas slid the blade across the open wound. Benjamin's body jerked, but he remained unconscious. The smell of burnt flesh permeated the air and both Annie and Lila ran from the cabin. Jenny felt lightheaded herself as perspiration beaded across her upper lip, but she remained stubbornly by Benjamin's side as Thomas applied some kind of poultice and wrapped the arm in clean bandages.

"Now what we gonna do?" Nathan wanted to know.

"We gonna wait," Thomas answered him impatiently. He rose from Benjamin's other side and retreated across the cabin, where he began to fix food for everyone. Jenny wondered just where this old man managed to get such an unending supply of goods.

When Thomas returned to check on Benjamin, Jenny asked him softly, "What we gonna do now, Uncle Thomas? Benjamin won't be able to travel fo' several days."

If he lives, she thought and began praying like she hadn't done since she was a child.

Thomas felt Benjamin's forehead, sighing in relief. "Least he ain't got no fever." He smiled at Jenny. "He'll make it, child. The Good Lord ain't finished with Benjamin Walters yet."

"The white man's God," Jenny murmured, unaware that she had spoken aloud.

Thomas snorted. "God ain't got no color, woman," he told her firmly. "Lessen it be yellow."

Surprised, Jenny glanced at his face. "Yellow?"

"God ain't like you and me. God is light. The Good Book say so. Now, what color would you say light is?"

Jenny noticed the morning sunlight beginning to filter into the cabin. As it passed through the window with its one pane, the light was reflected into a shimmering rainbow. Jenny smiled.

"I'd say light is *all* colors."

Thomas was delighted. "Smart girl!"

A God without color. The thought boggled Jenny's mind. In every picture she had ever seen of Jesus, He was always depicted as being white.

"What 'bout Jesus?" she asked the old man.

"You ever heard of a Jew?"

Jenny shook her head. "No."

"Well, the Jews be God's chosen people. As for color, they be brown. But it ain't their color what made them God's people. It were their heart." He studied her seriously. "The heart don' know no color, Jenny. Not if it's right wit God." He suddenly changed the subject. "Does you know how to read?"

"Yessir. Miss Adelaide taught me when I was a little girl, even though it was agin the law." Thinking of those fun times now, Jenny felt a pang at the things she had left behind without even a thought. She watched the others eating the food Thomas had prepared for them and wondered at their pasts. Amelia and Nathan she knew. But what about the others? She hadn't even taken the time to find out, so caught up was she in her own selfishness.

Thomas handed her a well-worn Bible. "Maybe you'd like to read some about God's people." He opened the Bible to the Book of Exodus. "You kin start here. But maybe you'd like to eat first."

She shook her head. "I'm not hungry."

Truth to tell, nothing would have moved her from Benjamin's side. Now she settled next to him and began to read, and she was soon caught up in the story of Moses and the Israelites. For a long time she read, impervious to the passing of time.

"Jenny."

She glanced up from her reading, marking the spot with her finger. Amelia stood beside her with a plate.

"You gots to eat somethin'."

Jenny smiled at her friend. "Thanks."

Taking the plate, she began to sop the redeye gravy with her biscuit. Amelia settled at her feet.

"Jasper and Annie been telling us 'bout everything. I been praying real hard for you."

"I been praying for you, too." Jenny was surprised at the truth of the statement. She *had* been praying for her friends. Even when she thought she didn't believe, she had often prayed for her friends and family.

Amelia smiled brightly. "Really? Praise the Lord." She motioned to Benjamin's still form. "What 'bout him?"

Instantly on the defensive at her friend's knowing look, Jenny asked with some asperity, "What 'bout him?"

"You loves him," Amelia stated with conviction.

For a moment Jenny was tempted to deny it, but Amelia knew her too well. They exchanged glances and Jenny sighed. It wasn't possible to love someone so quickly, was it?

"What makes you think that?" she asked, dipping her biscuit again to avoid her friend's searching gaze.

"It's in yo' eyes," Amelia told her softly.

Jenny continued eating, trying to think of something to say. She didn't want to acknowledge such feelings, even to herself. Saying the words would somehow make her committed. She caught Amelia's eyes, her own uncertain.

"Yes," she told her friend quietly. "I do."

Her eyes went back to Benjamin's face and she found him awake, his brown eyes boring into hers.

ten

Time ticked slowly by as Thomas tended to Benjamin's wound. Periodically, Benjamin's eyes would lock with Jenny's and she would hastily glance away to avoid the message she felt sure he was sending. She knew there would come a time of reckoning, but she just couldn't face him yet.

Obviously Benjamin had heard her declaration of love, but she hadn't stayed around long enough to find out what his reply would be. She hated to imagine what he must think of her. It was rather presumptuous of an ignorant, ragged woman to hope that such a sophisticated man of the world like Benjamin could return her feelings. She was afraid to look into his eyes for fear that she would read harsh thoughts about herself. This insecurity was a new feeling for her. She had always been so self-assured, even though she had been a slave. Probably because she had never seen herself as such, and that was due, no doubt, to the fact that she had never really been treated like one. These new feelings of inferiority were unsettling, to say the least.

For a moment she paused as her mind dwelt on that kiss by the river. Something intangible had passed between her and Benjamin, she was sure of it. Something that left her yearning for more. Unexpectedly she was filled with such longing that she thought she would burst.

❧

Benjamin's thoughts were running along parallel lines had Jenny but known it. He watched her move about the cabin, his thoughts in turmoil. Although his mental processes had been thrown into chaos at her innocent declaration, one thing stood out clearly in his mind. Jenny was not one to give her love lightly. She had reached the age of twenty-six without ever having committed her emotions to any man. He was awed that he had so received such favor, but at the same time he was also inclined to be dubious.

He was often the recipient of someone's affection when he was considered to be their savior. Even as a doctor he had had similar problems. Still, he had never felt about any woman the way he felt about Jenny. There was something extraordinary about the way they responded to one another. He could no more explain it than he could deny it.

In the end, he decided that he should ignore her confession until he had a full opportunity to do something about it. She was gradually moving her way toward a belief in the God of heaven, yet still she held back. Her feelings and words were somewhat paradoxical. At times he thought she was about ready to give herself to the Lord; at other times he could see that she just wanted to lash out at someone or something. Her faith, if she truly had any, was transient at best, and without a sound belief in God, Benjamin knew this woman could not be for him.

The best thing to do would be to avoid contact with her as much as possible until they were safe farther north. He knew it would be hard to do, but he hadn't developed a will of iron for nothing. If there was one thing he had acquired a surplus of over the last several years, it was patience. As long as Jenny herself continued to ignore him, he knew he could handle the situation. If, however, she once turned those fiery brown eyes his way, he knew he would be in big trouble.

❧

Jenny, blissfully unaware of his thoughts, was still busy with her own. Benjamin had such an unshakable faith in God, yet look what had happened to them thus far. Dawson was dead, Bill and Zeke had disappeared, and Benjamin had been shot. More and more she was convinced that the God Benjamin so worshipped was a God for white men. Benjamin's faith set them even farther apart than ever. They were from two different worlds, as far apart as night and day.

At times she wondered if Benjamin could have any feelings for her, but then she genuinely doubted it. Still, it was hard to shake the hope when they had shared that kiss by the river. Even now, thinking about it made her insides quiver.

When she chanced a look in his direction, she found him watching Amelia as she reclined next to Nathan. Jenny felt her stomach twist with jealousy, and then berated herself severely for it. There were no ties between Benjamin and herself. Besides, Amelia had eyes for no one but her Nate. Never had, never would.

Still, Benjamin eyed the two for a long while, his face clouded with suspicion. Something about the two obviously troubled him. Jenny had no idea what it could be until he finally spoke, his look focused on Nathan.

"I believe I owe you my thanks for saving my life."

Jenny was surprised when Nathan's face darkened with color and he quickly glanced away. "It weren't nothin'."

"We haven't been introduced, but I think I recognize your voice. You're Simon and Sarah, aren't you?"

Tension seemed to be stretched as tight as a clothesline between the two men. Unsure just what was causing it, Jenny vaulted to her feet and hastily intervened. "No. This here's Nate and Amelia. You know, the two I told you about."

Benjamin's frowning look centered on Nate again. "I know you're the same man who hit me. You told me your name was Simon and that Sarah was your wife."

Nathan looked truly flustered, his eyes going quickly from Benjamin to Jenny.

"I weren't sure 'bout you. I tole you, you didn't sound like no darkie. And in the dark I couldn't tell anything about you."

Jenny could see Benjamin relax back against the mattress. Relieved, Jenny took the time to introduce everyone. It would seem that misgivings were abundant on both sides. Even Jasper hadn't seemed inclined to believe Nathan's story. She was glad to be able to clear her friends of any suspicion. A niggling little thought refused to be dislodged from her mind, however. At least he hadn't been staring at Amelia because he was attracted to her.

Jenny seated herself next to Thomas at the table. Her eyes strayed from time to time to Benjamin, but she addressed herself to the old man. "What's gonna happen now, Thomas?"

He shrugged, concentrating on the splint he was trying to fashion for Benjamin's arm. "Don't rightly know. I 'spect we won't have no more trouble with trackers fo' a while. Words gonna git around 'bout them others, and it's gonna be some time 'fore others will try what they did."

Benjamin eased himself to a sitting position on the bed, slowly dropping his legs over the side. It took every ounce of will Jenny possessed not to rush to his aid.

"I agree," Benjamin told the room at large, beads of sweat dotting his brow. "Now would be the perfect time for us to leave."

Jenny was about to argue, but his next words stopped her cold. He searched each face carefully before returning his look to Lila, a frown creasing his brow. "Where's Bill and Zeke?"

All noise ceased in the small cabin as every eye focused on Benjamin. Jasper eyed him warily, obviously wondering, like Jenny, if that blow to the head had done more damage than they had at first supposed. "Don' you remember? They was lost in the river."

Benjamin studied them thoughtfully, his mind reaching for the information that was just out of his grasp. Images floated into his head of Bill and Zeke tied to a tree. Benjamin shook his head slowly, grimacing as pain shot through him at the movement.

"No. I saw them. Just before the shooting started."

Lila came to her feet, clutching Harriet tightly in her arms. For a moment, her surprised look was centered on Benjamin, but then her fierce gaze locked onto Nathan. "What you know 'bout that?"

Nathan looked even more astonished than Lila. "I don' know nothing. I didn't see no men tied to no tree."

"They were there," Benjamin reiterated. "I saw them both. I was trying to reach them when a stray bullet hit me and knocked me down."

When everyone looked to Nathan for confirmation, he just shrugged. "I didn't see no one else, 'cept bodies."

Lila's fearful stare focused on Nathan once again. Her eyes asked the question her lips refused to utter.

Nathan shook his head. "No. I checked the bodies. They be all white men."

"What'll happen to all them bodies?" Jenny asked, almost afraid of the answer.

"I don' know," Thomas told them sadly. "Usually, the vigilantes don' kill nobody. They just take slaves away from the trackers. Somethin' awful must of happened for them to be so brutal."

Benjamin remembered Dawson's face as it peered up at him from its earthen grave. Had that been the reason for the savage attack? Justice had been served, and yet he wouldn't have wished such deaths on anyone. And what of Bill and Zeke?

"What do you think will happen to Bill and Zeke?" he asked Thomas.

"I 'spect them vigilantes will git 'em to safety."

Lila moaned, dropping listlessly to the floor. She cuddled Harriet closer, tears running down her dark cheeks. "Oh, Bill! How we ever gonna find you?"

Benjamin could almost feel the anguish from the woman as she continued to rock her daughter. "We'll find them, Lila. At least we know they're alive!"

For a moment her visage drooped with sorrow, then ever so slowly, her lips curled up into a faltering smile as she eyed Benjamin. "That's true, Dr. Ben. And if anyone kin find 'em, you kin."

Feeling the weight of responsibility settle heavily on his shoulders, Benjamin sighed soundlessly. If it was within his power, he would make good on his word. But he knew that in the end, it would be *God's* will, not his own, that would triumph.

❧

They left early the next morning amid strenuous objections from Thomas. His concern for Benjamin's welfare was touching, but Benjamin had a job to do. He wasn't about to let a bullet slow him down when he knew this was a prime opportunity for travel.

The rest had done them all good, but Harriet was showing signs of having been in the damp, cold tunnel too long. She was running a slight fever and was in all probability developing a cold.

There were people in Indianapolis who would help them if they could only reach there safely, but they had a long way to go. Benjamin lifted his face to the cloudy sky and hastened his footsteps. In all probability it would rain before nightfall and that would do no one any good, least of all little Harriet.

The farther they went into Illinois, the less Benjamin feared for their safety. Trackers seldom traveled these woods, preferring to grab their prey when they arrived in the cities.

As they traveled, it became apparent to Benjamin that Jenny was avoiding him as much as possible, and although he had pretty much decided to do the same, he was still peeved at her evasion. He found himself watching her when he should have been studying the terrain around them.

Jenny could feel his eyes on her as she stumbled along the uneven ground, and she wondered what he could possibly be thinking that caused his eyes to gleam in such a fashion. His attraction was so powerful, she felt like a helpless moth against a candle's flame. Not liking the feeling, she set her shoulders firmly; lifting her chin with determination, she refused to look his way again.

They soon came upon a small farm, and although it wasn't a regular station on the Railroad, the white occupants were sympathetic to their cause. The farmer allowed them free use of his barn, and after a time his wife brought them some food.

"It ain't much," she told them, "but it's all we got to spare."

The travelers dug into the food after Benjamin asked God's

blessing on it. The fluffy biscuits were filling, and the chicken stew was warm and sufficient to fill their hungry bellies. Only little Harriet remained unsatisfied.

Since Benjamin no longer feared detection, he had refrained from using the paregoric. As the babe continued to squirm and fret, he placed a hand on her forehead, pulling it away with a frown. The child was ill, and no mistake. If her cold went into her lungs, she could develop pneumonia and die.

They were still a long way from Indianapolis and there were only small towns between here and there. He needed to find one with a railroad.

Carefully he measured a small amount of medicine to relieve the child of her fever. She choked on the tonic as he tried to massage it down her throat. Laying a hand against her small cheek, Benjamin was surprised when the infant turned and latched onto his thumb, sucking as though her life depended on it. He found Lila watching him.

"I think I ain't got enough milk, Dr. Ben."

So busy had his thoughts been, Benjamin hadn't considered this possibility. Sighing, he patted Lila's hand where it rested against Harriet's back.

"It's probably from your poor diet. At times we have enough, at others we almost starve."

Hearing their conversation, Jenny crossed the barn to their side. "They's a milk cow here."

Benjamin's eyes followed Jenny's look across to a stall in the far corner. Perhaps the owners would allow him some milk for the baby. Rising to his feet, he told Lila, "I'll be back in a minute. I'm going to ask the farmer if we can have some milk."

"How we gonna feed it to her?" Lila wanted to know.

Benjamin wasn't certain, but if he had to, he would use a medicine dropper and feed the child all night.

After he left, Jenny sat down beside Lila, crossing her legs Indian style. "You want me to take her fo' awhile?"

Relieved, Lila handed her fussing daughter to Jenny. She smiled her appreciation. "I don' know if it'll do any good fo' her, but I shore could use the rest."

Jenny lifted Harriet over her shoulder and began to rock back and forth, crooning a song her mama had sung to her many years ago. Before long the baby's cries slackened to whimpering as Jenny continued to massage her tiny back.

It wasn't long before Benjamin returned with a bottle of milk. Surprised, Jenny looked him in the eye for the first time in days. Benjamin grinned back at her.

"Now tell me the Lord doesn't provide! This family had a baby calf born last year and the mama died, so they had to feed it by bottle. That's what took me so long. I had to wait while she sterilized it."

Lila took the bottle from him, her mouth parted slightly. Her features wore the same look of wonder as did Benjamin's at this unexpected blessing.

Jenny handed the child back to her mother and got to her feet, refusing to meet either pair of eyes. Her brow was creased in thought as she walked away from them. Some things truly did seem amazing and, at times, it really did seem as though Benjamin's God was looking out for them. But what about the bad things? Did the good outweigh the bad?

Benjamin watched Jenny climb the ladder to the loft and heard her rustle among the hay. He hadn't missed the skeptical look she had thrown him, and although he had promised himself that he would stay away from her, he couldn't let this opportunity pass.

He mounted the ladder, stopping as his head and shoulders reached above the top. It was dark up here, and it took him a moment to find where Jenny had sat down among the straw. A shaft of moonlight came through the loft's closed doors, lighting the area where she sat. He finished climbing up into the loft and stood over her, his hands resting on his hips.

"Mind if I join you?"

She brushed at the straw clinging to her hair. "Is somethin' wrong? I. . .I'm kinda tired."

"I just wanted to talk to you a minute."

Aggravated, Jenny ducked her head to avoid his searching look. After almost two weeks with barely a word, now he wanted to talk to her, and she was almost certain she knew what was on his mind.

"What about?"

Without waiting for permission, he settled himself beside her. Although he was watching her, Jenny kept her face averted.

After a moment, Benjamin reached out and pulled several strands of hay from her hair. Jenny could feel her heart start to pound as his breath fanned softly across her cheek. Somehow she didn't think that this little talk in such close proximity was a good idea.

"Jenny, look at me."

The moonlight shimmered around them, softly illuminating the area where they were sitting. His velvety voice sent a little flutter of excitement running through her. Reluctantly, she did as she was bid. Expecting censure, she found only sympathy in his dark mahogany eyes.

"Why don't you trust God?" he asked her gently.

Even in the dimness, Benjamin could see the closed expression come to her face. She turned away, but he firmly took her by the chin and turned her back.

"Talk to me, Jenny."

She jerked her chin from his grasp, but continued to stare him in the eye. He could see the anger shining there.

"You say God takes care of us, but Dawson's dead, and goodness only knows what happened to Bill and Zeke!" Her eyes focused on his bandaged shoulder. "And what 'bout you? You who love God and serve Him. How He repay you fo' your service? He let you git shot, that's how!"

Benjamin shook his head slowly. "No, Jenny. You've got it all wrong."

She started to rise to her feet, but Benjamin took her by the wrist and refused to let go.

"Sit down and listen to me for a minute."

"I don' wanna."

"Well, do it anyway."

There was something so inflexible about the set of his broad shoulders that Jenny knew she wasn't going anywhere. She settled back, glaring at his hand where it still shackled her wrist. He released her, his look never once leaving her face.

"I love God because He *is* God. I worship Him because He's worthy of worship. I don't love Him because I'm afraid of Him, and I don't worship Him to see what I can get out of Him. I love and worship Him because *He is God!* "

She frowned. "I don' understand."

Sighing, Benjamin searched his mind for a way to explain. He studied her puzzled face before finally alighting on an idea.

"Jenny, do you love your papa?"

Her eyes gleamed fiercely in the darkness. "Course I love him. I don' love no one as much as my pappy, 'cept maybe my mama."

"And did your father ever punish you?"

"Course he did. Everyone's folks punish them."

He could see that she was struggling to follow his reasoning. He leaned forward to see her face better, his hand covering hers where it lay against the straw.

"Did your father ever let something bad happen to you that you didn't understand at the time?"

Jenny thought back to the time when she was just a little girl of six. Even then she had a stubborn streak that refused to bow to authority. Mama and Pappy had told her so many times to leave the stove in the big house alone, but rebelliously she had refused to listen. Finally, Pappy had stood back and allowed her to touch the forbidden item.

Jenny glanced down at the faint scar on her palm. Pappy's tears had mixed with her own as she had screamed in pain, but never again did she go near the stove. And from that time on, she was also reluctant to disobey Pappy.

She told Benjamin the story and he nodded his head knowingly. "And did you hate your father? Turn your back on him?"

"No." Although her head was bowed, he could see that she

understood where he was going with this conversation.

"Tell me, Jenny. Where is your father now? Why isn't he here to take care of you?"

Angry tears sparkled in her eyes as they meshed with his. " 'Cause I ran away!"

"So because he isn't here to take care of you, you don't love him anymore?"

She leaned forward and impaled him with a look that would have quailed a lesser man. "I'll always love my pappy!" she declared vehemently. "It ain't his fault I ran away."

"Why?" Benjamin pressed. "Why do you love him?"

In an instant, she was on her feet, her hands planted firmly on her hips. "Because he's my pappy, that's why!"

"And that's why I love my heavenly Father," he told her softly. "Just because He *is* my Father. Not because He cares for me, though He does. Not because I'm afraid of Him, though I am. Not because I think I should, but just because *He is*."

Jenny dropped slowly back to the hay, her mind a confusion of thoughts.

"If you went home right now," Benjamin asked her, "what would your father do?"

Barely able to speak around the lump in her throat, Jenny's voice came out a hoarse whisper. "He would hug me and kiss me and cry over me."

Benjamin reached forward and gripped her hand tightly. "Your heavenly Father would do the same thing. Even the angels in heaven would sing praise. You've been running away from God as much as your pappy. They both want you to come home."

Benjamin could see her reluctance to give in. He placed a palm against her cheek. "I love God just because He is God, and He loves me for the same reason. Just because I'm me. His child, as unworthy as I am. Someday I will have children of my own, God willing, and I will love them unconditionally just because they *are* my children. Even if they turn their back on me, I will still love them."

Jenny covered the hand that still clutched hers with her other hand, her gaze flickering over his face. "But you *loves* God. Why He don't protect you better?"

"I don't know the reason, just as you didn't know why your pappy let you get sick. But there *was* a reason. Unlike you, I may never understand why, but I still believe there was a reason."

Jenny felt his words settle into her heart and wrap warmly around her like a cocoon. Benjamin took a small book from his pocket. Holding the Bible out to her, he told her, "Job loved God because He *was* God. Satan questioned that love, believing that Job only loved God because of what He provided. It's a powerful story. Read it."

He started to get up, but Jenny held him in place.

"Benjamin?"

There was an imploring timbre to her voice, a sultry quality that sent his pulse drumming through his veins. An unconscious fire in her eyes provoked an answering spark in his own. He took a deep breath and moved away from her.

"Don't tempt me, Jenny," he told her huskily, and she blushed, knowing that she had unwittingly invited his censure.

Although Jenny would never have believed otherwise, it took an immense effort on Benjamin's part to leave her sitting there.

❧

Jenny watched him go, her heart shattering into a thousand pieces. For a brief moment she had felt a wildness she didn't even know she possessed. She had wanted Benjamin to take her in his arms and never let her go. To tell her that he loved her. She wanted his passion to match her own. His rejection left her feeling frozen inside and out.

Ashamed of herself, she pushed away the Bible and threw herself into the hay, burying her sobs against her arms. How could she have tested Benjamin that way, especially after his having shared God's love for her? Why had her thoughts and feelings settled upon the man instead of his message? In her heart she knew she had been wrong to entice him that way, but a reckless part of her didn't care. Since meeting Benjamin, her feelings had been in constant turmoil, and for the first time in her life, she craved a relationship with a man. She was finally beginning to realize that it was possible for her to have the kind of companionship that her parents shared, but she was unsure how to go about having one. Never having experienced anything like this situation, she found herself making rash mistakes.

Rolling over, she dried her eyes on her sleeve and forced her mind to think of other things. Years of discipline worked to quickly suppress any thoughts she didn't desire.

Regardless of how Benjamin felt about her, he had given her much to think about. She had never thought to love God just because He *was* God. As she thought about it, she realized that that was exactly how her parents believed. For whatever reason they were put upon this earth, they trusted God to work according to His divine plan. Could she learn to trust like that? How did one acquire that kind of faith?

Closing her eyes, she prayed until her thoughts stilled and her body relaxed. Before long, she fell into a deep sleep.

eleven

After two days of weary travel, Benjamin finally called a halt. Although the sun was warm, November was just a few short days away, and the ambient air temperature was chilling as they traveled through the stark forests. Crunching their way through a thick carpet of maple and oak leaves, intermingled with hickory and black walnut, the dense branches above them, although bare, allowed very little sunlight to filter through.

Benjamin checked little Harriet once again, his concern growing at the child's increasing temperature. There was nothing he could do, except try to make the little girl as comfortable and warm as possible—a near impossibility since cold Canadian air had swept through the region. Thomas had insisted that it was going to be a long, cold winter since the animal pelts were thicker than normal, but Benjamin hadn't really given it much thought. Until now.

They traveled during the day now that they were farther into Illinois, but the nights had grown extremely cold. Although Benjamin feared for their safety, they had no choice except to build a fire. Without some warmth, they all might become ill.

The sun had started its evening descent and already the temperatures were dropping. Jenny made her way to Benjamin's side, her concern etched across her face. "Are we stopping here, Benjamin?"

Benjamin had noticed that the longer Jenny traveled in his company, the more she talked like him. Obviously, she was trying to learn and grow.

Since that night in the barn, she had studiously avoided him, and he had made it easier for her by doing the same thing. Even now, just the thought of her suggestive voice warmed his blood.

She must really be concerned to have sought him out without the safety of the others. He dropped his pack and began to gather some dry brush and twigs for a fire. Little Harriet's dry, racking cough came clearly to them as he continued his work.

When Jenny finally managed to look into Benjamin's face, she found his own worry mirrored hers.

"How bad is she, Benjamin?"

Feeling helpless, Benjamin threw down his load of sticks and drew a match from his pack. "Pretty bad." His eyes met Jenny's and he read the fear there. "We *have* to get to a shelter soon. I didn't want to go farther tonight because we aren't far from the Wabash River, but another night in the open with the cold winds isn't going to do her any good."

Jenny glanced around. "Isn't there anywhere we could go?"

"Not that I'm aware of. We're farther south than I usually travel. Normally I go farther north and try to reach South Bend without having to cross the Wabash, but I'm afraid it might be too late if I do that."

Jenny followed his look across to the log where Lila was trying desperately to keep Harriet warm and comforted. Lila drew the bottle from her pack and nudged it into her daughter's mouth. For a time, quiet reigned in the woods as the baby sucked hungrily at the milk. Although they had filled several canteens with cow's milk, the milk wouldn't last much longer.

Heart melting at the sight, Jenny turned back to Benjamin. "What you gonna do?"

"For right now, I'm going to build a fire."

Jenny sensed his anger, but she knew that it was self-directed. "It's not your fault, Benjamin."

Benjamin's head snapped up, his eyes as chilling as the cool night air. He said nothing, just turned back to the fire that was growing steadily as he threw on more wood.

The wall that Benjamin had thrown up between them was thicker than the forest trees, and Jenny sighed with frustration. She truly wanted to help him, but she wasn't certain how to go about it. Benjamin's mood had grown steadily more morose with each passing day. She was fairly certain that he was blaming himself for all the problems they had encountered and for the loss of the others.

Jenny wanted to talk to Benjamin about his God, assure him that He was watching over them just as Benjamin believed He was, but she truly doubted it. Maybe it was true what the white preacher had said. Maybe slaves *were* supposed to be content to be slaves and serve their masters faithfully. What was that Scripture he had used? Something about slaves obeying their earthly masters. Maybe that was why all these disasters had fallen upon them. And now it was possible that little Harriet might be their next casualty.

Jenny went and sat next to Lila, her eyes following Benjamin as he made his rounds asking each of them about their day. Were there any sore throats? Was anyone feeling ill? Did they need anything?

And if they did? Just what was *he* supposed to do about it? Could he produce warm blankets from thin air? Could he whip up a filling meal? Her anger increased the more she thought about it. He wasn't God, so why should he feel responsible for everything?

Lila's shoulders slumped with fatigue, and without hesitation Jenny reached out and took Harriet from her arms. There were tears in Lila's amber eyes when they lifted to Jenny's. Jenny squeezed her hand reassuringly.

"It'll be okay. Benjamin won't let anything happen to Harriet."

"It ain't that what bothers me most." Her look dropped to the baby. "She be okay iffen. . .iffen, well, iffen anything happen to her. The Good Lord, He take care of my baby, either here or there."

Confused, Jenny asked, "Then what's bothering you?"

Sniffing, Lila wiped her eyes on her sleeve. "My Bill, he only seen his baby fo' one day. He only gots to hold her one time."

Jenny didn't know what to say. She pulled her knees up to

her chest and thought it might be best if she changed the subject. Without looking at Lila, she prompted, "Lila, tell me about you."

Puzzled, Lila asked her, "What you mean?"

"Why did you and Bill run away? Where'd you run away from?"

A sad look crossed the young mother's features. "Bill and me, we come from Tennessee."

Surprised, Jenny interrupted, "Me, too!"

Lila said nothing, just nodded her head. "Bill and me, we jumped the broom 'bout two years ago. Course our massa, he don't take no stock of such things. He don't allow his slaves to marry, but in our hearts, me and Bill is just as married as if we had a preacher."

Jenny lifted the fussing Harriet to her shoulder and began the rhythmic rubbing of her back that seemed to settle the child down.

"Our massa," Lila continued, "was one of the rich ones. They ain't too many of 'em, but they's enough!"

"Were you ever beat?"

"Sometimes. The first overseer we had was a good man. Because he treated us good, we made sho' we worked good fo' him. Sometimes he would beat a fence post 'stead of us and we would yell like we was dying." Her lips curled up at the memory, her eyes staring off into the distance. Suddenly the smile disappeared and her eyes became almost feral in their intensity.

"Then the massa gots a new overseer and he were a *mean* man. Sometimes he beat the slaves fo' nothing. He beat me one time when he caught me and Bill kissing." Her face flooded with color, and she dropped her eyes shyly.

"Is that why you ran away?"

Lila shook her head, her eyes sparking angrily. "No. After me and Bill jumped the broom, we still couldn't live together. It were hard fo' both of us, but harder fo' Bill. Massa Jessop, he sometimes lent the slaves to other folks, mainly what I heard the massa say was "yeoman farmers," whatever that mean. I just know they was different. Those massas used to work in the fields right along wit the slaves."

Harriet had finally fallen asleep and Jenny handed her gently back into her mother's waiting arms. She studied Lila curiously. "You mean the master actually worked in the *fields*?"

"Mmm, hmmm. These yeoman farmers didn't have enough money to keep lots of slaves. They needed as many hands in the fields as possible."

Jenny had a hard time imagining such a thing. She tried, but failed, to picture Mr. Greer doing such a thing. Jenny didn't think Amelia's pot-bellied master had ever worked a day in his life. As for Mr. Jackson, her own master, she supposed he might have worked hard in his younger years, but she really didn't know. Her reflections were interrupted as Lila continued.

"The thing what made us leave was when the massa started lending Bill to other massas to give 'em more little slaves. Bill and me, we be Christians. When Bill supposed to sleep with another woman, he just couldn't do it. The women, they understood. They would pretend that Bill did sleep wit them, but he really sleep on the floor." Lila shuddered. "Then the overseer, he found out 'bout it and whipped Bill good, but Bill, he just tell that ole Mr. Hooper that he were a Christian and that it were wrong to sleep wit a woman you not married to."

Jenny felt her face flame with embarrassment when she thought about the way she had acted in that barn loft. She hoped the others weren't aware of her shameful actions. "Is that why you ran away?"

Lila nodded, her gaze resting briefly on Jenny's troubled features. "Mr. Hooper told Bill that iffen he didn't do what he was told, he would beat *me*, or worse, sell Bill down South."

Jenny's eyes flew to Amelia sitting next to Nathan. Her story was very similar. As for Jenny herself, her own story was much different. She had never been beaten, never gone hungry, never went without proper clothing. She had it so much better than these two women, and yet they believed in

God so strongly that it put Jenny to shame.

"Why you believe in God, Lila?"

The look of astonishment on Lila's face caused Jenny's shame to deepen.

"Don' you believe in the Lord, Jenny?"

Jenny couldn't bring herself to meet the other woman's eyes. "I. . .I suppose. But I don't see why we should. Everyone tells me that He ain't just a white man's God, but I don't see Him doing too much to help us."

Distressed, Lila laid her hand on Jenny's arm. "I don' know what to say. I ain't got all the answers, I just *know* that there's a God. Bill told me one time that iffen the whites hadn't brought us here as slaves, none of us would have ever known Jesus."

Snorting, Jenny bit her lip to keep from hurling an invective that would have shocked the other woman. Surely there was a better way to reach the blacks than bringing them as slaves to America.

"What about Bill and Zeke and Dawson?" Jenny's blazing eyes went to the sleeping Harriet. "And what about Harriet? Why didn't God take better care of 'em?"

"Jenny," Lila remonstrated softly. "God *did* take care of Bill and Zeke. And little Harriet ain't dead yet." Her wry smile reprimanded Jenny more than words could have.

"I'm sorry, you're right. And if Benjamin has anything to do with it, she won't."

Lila agreed. "And as fo' Dawson. It weren't God told him to try to kill them white men."

"What?" Jenny's mahogany eyes rounded in surprise.

Nodding, Lila continued. "Yep. Nate and Amelia saw it. Even though he were well hidden and couldn't be seen, Dawson jumped on one of the men and tried to kill him."

Shocked, Jenny couldn't find her voice to speak. Her head slowly moved from side to side as she tried to take in this new information. Did Benjamin know? And if so, why hadn't he mentioned it?

"There's a story from the Bible that I heard a preacher tell one Sunday," Lila told Jenny. "It's about two men what built a house. One built it on the sand, and one built it on the rock."

Jenny had heard that story also. "I know. The rock be Jesus."

"That's true," Lila agreed. "But even though he built his house on Jesus, the storm, the wind, and the rain *still* came. Building his house on Jesus didn't keep him safe from the storm, but it did keep him from falling when the storm came. Jesus, He keep us safe. Even the 'postles were killed, but they were still safe in God's arms."

Benjamin's voice snapped Jenny out of her preoccupation. "We need to get some sleep." He handed Lila his jacket. "Wrap this around Harriet. It will help keep her warm."

Surprised, Lila tried to argue. "That don't leave you with nothin'. You'll freeze, Dr. Ben."

"I'll be okay. I'll stay close to the fire. Don't argue, Lila."

As with the others, Lila was quick to obey, although Jenny could tell she didn't appreciate it.

"We'll start out early," Benjamin informed everyone.

When Jenny's eyes met his, she couldn't read past the veil he seemed to have erected. Her own eyes dropped to her blanket and then lifted back to his face. She opened her mouth to recommend that they share, but before the words could even leave her mouth, he told her implacably, "Don't even suggest it."

Jenny's lips set into a mutinous line as she watched him walk away. She had only meant to help! *Fine. Let the man freeze!*

When she happened to glance at Lila, the other woman smiled knowingly before curling into a ball close to the fire and snuggling Harriet securely against her. Jenny watched Benjamin sit down across from her next to the fire, her mind a confusing mass of anger, shame, and other feelings she couldn't quite put a name to. Refusing to give in to such emotions, Jenny lay down close to Lila, trying to create a warmer nest for little Harriet. It took some time before her eyes finally closed in sleep.

❧

When they awakened in the morning, the ground was hidden beneath a thick layer of mist. The bare trees rose eerily from a dense fog that came from the river in the distance. Shivering, the party was quick to decamp and start the trek for the waters of the Wabash.

Benjamin was uncertain what he would find, but he knew there were settlements along this river. He still hoped to be able to find one that had the railroad running through. It was imperative that he get Lila and the baby to Indianapolis. He had friends there that would keep them both safe until the child was well, and then they would help the two get to freedom.

The closer he got to his destination, the more his mind was in a turmoil about what to do with Jenny. She was determined to go to Canada, and he couldn't blame her, but his own destiny lay elsewhere.

He hadn't meant to eavesdrop, but when he had heard Lila and Jenny talking about God, he couldn't bring himself to interrupt. He was amazed that as uneducated as Lila was, she had an infinitely better grasp on Christianity than most people. Her faith was genuine and came from deep within. He couldn't have given a better sermon himself.

But what had Jenny thought about Lila's teaching? What was going through that crazy woman's head now? He didn't think if he had a hundred years he would ever be able to figure Jenny out.

If Jenny ever gave her life to God, that would be the end of it. There would be no turning back for her, she was that stubborn in her beliefs. Was she any closer to believing than when they had first been introduced?

She made no bones about her feelings for Benjamin. A deep attraction pulled between the two, as great as any magnetic force he had ever encountered. At times Jenny would reach out to him, at others she held him away. He couldn't blame her, really. His own actions had surely helped to confuse her. One minute hot, the next cold. He found it a daily struggle to keep to the path he had ordered for his life. He wanted so much to be close to Jenny. To touch her. But at other times, he remembered the admonition of the Scriptures not to be unequally yoked with unbelievers.

It was imperative that he refocus on the Lord. Every thought, every action, should be for Him. Out here among the forests and rivers it was easy to forget that there were any rules. His eyes rested on a jay flitting among the trees. Surely such beautiful scenery must be close to that of the first Eden. If there was no serpent in *this* garden, there was certainly a tempting apple.

His gaze fastened on Jenny again as she relieved Lila of little Harriet's wiggling body. It amazed him that Jenny seemed to have grown from the somber, aloof young lady he had at first encountered to a friendly, helpful young woman. Harriet adored her, and watching Jenny playing with the baby, he could well understand why.

Still, that didn't help him with his problem. Had God brought Jenny into his life only to have her leave after taking his heart? Sighing, he finally admitted it to himself. He was flat in love with the woman, and there was no longer any denying it. He had been attracted to enough women in the past to know that this was different. Now what was he supposed to do about it?

❧

The quiet plantation morning was broken by the sound of thundering hooves. Adam Jackson strode from his house to find the cause of this early morning intrusion. His overseer, Daniel Pearson, met him at the bottom of the marble stairs. Both men turned simultaneously to face Jeremiah Hawkins sitting boldly between the sheriff and his deputy. An armed posse of about twenty men surrounded the group.

Hawkins's lips curled into a sneer as he fixed the two men with a glaring look. "Ain't so high and mighty, now, are you, Adam Jackson."

Adam ignored the man, fixing his look on the sheriff. "What's this all about?"

The man cleared his throat before glancing hesitantly from Adam to Hawkins. "We need to search your place, Mr. Jackson. We're looking for a runaway."

"There aren't any runaways here. I told Mr. Hawkins that several weeks ago."

Hawkins spit a wad of tobacco juice, barely missing Adam's polished boots. "That was then, this is now."

The sheriff glared at the crusty overseer before turning back to Adam. "Excuse me, Mr. Jackson, but you would be doing us a big favor if you would allow us to at least search. Things are really heating up farther north, and there's talk of South Carolina seceding from the union. This has inspired the abolitionists to increase their networking, and we have cause to believe that there's a station somewhere around here."

Adam took a deep breath before turning to the overseer. "And what has this to do with you, Hawkins?"

Narrowed eyes glared balefully back at Adam Jackson. "This here slave is one of Greer's. One of the best studs he's got. We can't afford to lose him."

Frowning with distaste, Adam turned his look back to the sheriff. "By all means, suh, search the plantation. But I warn you," again his eyes fixed on Hawkins, "you had better not harass my slaves."

At a nod from the sheriff, the other men dismounted and spanned out across the grounds. Hawkins stayed seated upon his horse, his look fixed steadily on Adam.

"I hear you got a runaway, too, Jackson."

Not by so much as a muscle twinge did Adam acknowledge the man's words.

"Yessir," he continued. "I hear she disappeared the night Amelia and Nathan did."

The sheriff fixed his look on Adam. "Do you have a runaway, Mr. Jackson?'

Adam shrugged. "Not at all. And what has that to do with you anyway?"

"Mr. Jackson, are you helping runaway slaves?"

"I am not."

The sheriff's look was serious. "If we find out you're lying, Mr. Jackson, I'll have to arrest you."

Hawkins spit on the ground again. "Penalty for helping runaways is death in this county, you know."

Aggravated, Adam told the sheriff, "Why don't you take your men and leave now. It's obvious you're not going to find what you want here."

Already the men were returning, shaking their heads at the sheriff's inquiry. The sheriff mounted his horse. When he turned to Adam again, he nodded briefly. "Remember what I said, Mr. Jackson."

As the others reined their horses about, Hawkins kept his facing the plantation owner.

"I'm heading north tomorrow. There was a raid by vigilantes on a tracking party. Friend of mine was killed. Maybe you know him? Shaun Mercer?"

Adam's lips pressed tightly together. He had heard of the man. Mercer was a notorious transporter of slaves, returning them to captivity after they had achieved freedom in the North. He was ruthless when dealing with darkies.

"What has that to do with me, Hawkins?"

The man snickered. "Just thought I'd keep a lookout for that runaway of yourn. Maybe I'll find her for you."

The suggestive tone wasn't lost on Adam. It took every ounce of will he possessed to keep his hands off the overseer.

"Actually, I'm looking for a big, black man that Shaun told me about. Says this fellow took away his slave coffle at gunpoint. Spoke with a Yankee accent."

There was a question behind the words.

"I wouldn't know anything about that," Adam asserted.

Hawkins's lips twisted into a grin. "Maybe not, but it's possible your runaway is with him. If I find her, I'll try real hard to get her back in one piece for you."

With these parting words, Hawkins jerked his horse around

and galloped after the others, his venomous laugh ringing eerily on the morning air. When Adam looked up, he found old Jeb watching the man's retreating back.

For a moment their eyes locked, Jeb's full of fear, Adam's full of sympathy. Turning away, the old man walked off, his shoulders hunched as though with a heavy weight.

twelve

By the time the group reached the river, the sun had already burned away the morning mists. Benjamin decided to follow the river north, because he realized that there would be towns along the waterway. He wasn't quite certain of the group's location, but he decided that they must be a few miles south of Terre Haute.

The railroad ran through Terre Haute, and it might be possible to ferret some of his passengers to safety among the various trains heading north. He had no idea if there was an Underground Railroad station in Terre Haute or not, but it was still his best chance of getting the others to safety.

They hadn't traveled far when they came upon a keelboat tied to the shore. The flatboat bobbed gently on the water, apparently abandoned. There was no sign of life, but the boat was fully loaded.

Warily Benjamin moved in closer to check it out, leaving the others safely in the barren trees not far from the shore. Hesitantly he climbed aboard.

"Is anyone here?"

The only answer he received was the sound of two squirrels chattering among the treetops.

He entered the narrow boxlike cabin at its center. Signs of habitation could be seen by the remains of a meal left half-eaten on the small table. Someone had obviously left in a hurry.

A ledger on the table drew Benjamin's attention and he picked it up, hoping for some information.

"That's a good way to git yourself killed, boy."

Startled, Benjamin dropped the book. He whirled to find a huge man standing in the doorway, his red beard and scraggly hair giving him a wild appearance.

Benjamin straightened, eyeing the man carefully. "I'm sorry. I was hoping to find out what had happened to the crew of this boat."

"They're around," the big man answered. His look ran briefly over Benjamin before he ambled farther into the small compartment.

"Are you the captain?" Benjamin asked.

The man snickered. "Flatboats ain't got *captains,* but I *am* the owner." His smile didn't quite reach his eyes. "You a runaway?"

"No."

"Didn't think so. You don't sound like any darkie I've ever known, 'cept maybe one. He's a ship's captain from New York." His eyes narrowed as they studied Benjamin. "I'm a *friend.*"

Although Benjamin recognized the code word that established those sympathetic to the abolition cause, he was reluctant to be forthcoming with a stranger.

"Why are you here?"

For the first time, laughter glimmered in the man's green eyes. "Well now, that's the problem. We had horses on board and one of 'em broke loose. Dove right into the water! We had to pull up here and try to git him back. My men took the other horses and lit out after the mangy beast, but I came on back to make sure my boat was safe."

The big man read the uncertainty in Benjamin's eyes. "Don't believe me, huh? Well, it's the truth. Take it or leave it. Anyway," he reached out a large hand, "name's Angus Morton."

Slowly Benjamin extended his own hand until it was engulfed by the other's beefy palm.

"My name is Benjamin Walters. I'm from Philadelphia."

Too late Benjamin realized his mistake.

"Long way from home, ain't you?"

"I. . .I had business here."

"Here? In the middle of nowhere?" Angus's look was

skeptical, but Benjamin remained silent. "Well, never mind," Angus continued. "Are you hungry?"

Benjamin was. Ravenously so, but he didn't want to admit it.

Angus seated himself at the only chair in the small compartment. His twinkling eyes went from Benjamin to the food on the table. "It ain't much, but you're welcome to share."

Relaxing slightly, Benjamin lifted a piece of bread from a plate. "Thanks."

Wanting to get back to the others quickly, Benjamin tried to find out if Angus was truly a "friend" or not. Before he could think of a question, Angus asked one of his own.

"You say you're from Philadelphia? You know a man named Thomas Dorsey?"

Surprised, Benjamin answered evasively. "I've heard of him."

"Well, he's a *friend* of mine. We've done business together a time or two."

Benjamin quirked an eyebrow. "What kind of business?"

"Oh, transportation mainly. You know, dry goods and hardware."

At the two code words, Benjamin felt his guard slip. Only those involved intimately with the abolitionist movement knew most of the passwords. Dry goods stood for black men, and hardware for black women.

Thomas Dorsey was a black caterer in Philadelphia who, along with Henry Jones and Henry Minton, fairly ruled the upper crust of society in Philadelphia through their stomachs. Their expertise with food had gained them a reputation that transcended social castes. All three were wealthy, but Thomas was the one most involved in the cause.

"What has that to do with me, Mr. Morton?"

Angus shrugged his shoulders, pursing his lips at the same time. "Just wondered if you might need a ride."

"Are you going upriver or down?"

"Well, I was going down, but I might be persuaded to go the other way if I had a good reason."

"What about your men?"

The big man chuckled. "My men are my sons. We go where *I* say."

Thinking rapidly, Benjamin made a decision. Little Harriet *had* to get to Indianapolis as soon as possible.

"Tell me, Mr. Morton. Do you know any of the *stations* in Indianapolis?"

Green eyes twinkling, Angus nodded. "Couple of fine ones."

"Well, I have some hardware that really needs to get there as quickly as possible. This hardware needs to go to a doctor's office. Do you think you can get it there?"

Angus's expression became serious. "Can do, but Terre Haute is closer. Couple of fine stations there, too."

Relieved, Benjamin moved to the door. "I'll be right back."

❧

When he explained the situation to Lila, he was surprised at her emphatic refusal.

"We don' know this man. He might be lying."

"I don't think so, Lila."

"What makes you so sure?" Jenny asked him, fearful for Lila and the baby.

His eyes met hers, and Jenny swallowed hard. Whenever his eyes took on that copper sheen, she knew he was fired with determination.

"I saw a Bible open on the table."

"That's it?" Jenny demanded. "That's enough for you to risk two lives?"

Lila's soft voice answered her. "It's enough for me."

Searching both faces, Jenny finally had to admit defeat. There was no way she could fight the two of them. Her heart twisted at the thought of losing little Harriet.

Lila gathered her things together, handing Benjamin back his jacket. He turned to the others.

"The rest of you stay put. I'll be back as soon as I get Lila settled."

Jenny watched them until they disappeared from sight, her

heart heavy at the loss of the two who had become almost like family to her. Amelia placed a loving arm around her waist.

"They will be okay, Jenny. The Good Lord will take care of them."

Surprisingly, Jenny was beginning to believe that herself. Nodding, she stood resolutely waiting for Benjamin to return.

❧

Five days later the weary pilgrims reached Terre Haute. Although Angus had offered to transport them all, the little keelboat would have been much too crowded, and with that many blacks aboard, much too suspicious.

Angus, however, was waiting for them when they trudged into town late that night.

"Thought you might make it today. Come with me."

Too tired to argue, they followed the bearded giant until he reached a small building in the center of town. The brightly lit windows were a beacon of encouragement. Angus knocked once, then twice.

After a moment they could hear someone on the other side of the door.

"Who is it?"

"A friend with some friends."

The door swung open quickly and a diminutive lady with curling white hair smiled up at Angus. "Come in, Angus."

"I can't stay, Bea. I have to get back, but I know my friends here will be in good hands."

After he left, they all huddled in her entryway. Bea's sympathetic look went from one to the other.

"Come in. You must be tired to death."

Benjamin stepped forward. "Lila?"

The woman smiled broadly. "Lila is fine, and so is little Harriet. She's just the cutest little thing!"

A man joined them, rolling down his shirt sleeves. Although he was advanced in years, his bearing was that of a much younger man. "What have we here?"

The woman motioned him forward. "This is my husband,

Dr. Mitchell. Honey, these are the friends Lila was telling us about."

"Where is Lila?" Jenny asked, unable to contain herself any longer.

Mrs. Mitchell suggested that they all go into the parlor. She sat down next to her husband, beaming at everyone. "Lila is on her way to Philadelphia."

Stunned, Benjamin came to his feet. "What?"

The doctor relaxed back against the sofa next to his wife. "You needn't worry, son. We knew of a train that would get her there without any problems. I've wired people along the way, and they will make sure nothing happens to her."

Jenny moved to the edge of her seat. "And Harriet?"

Looking puzzled, Mrs. Mitchell answered, "Why, Harriet's with her, of course."

"But is she well?"

"Oh my goodness, yes. Dr. Mitchell tended her cold and we fed them and gave them warm clothes. We promised to keep an eye out for her Bill and his father."

The doctor got to his feet. "We'll get you folks cleaned up and fed, and then we can discuss plans."

❧

Later that night, Jenny lay on her pallet, her mind in a spin. The doctor had arranged passage for all of them. Jenny was to go by train to Philadelphia, Jasper by flatboat as a crewman to the same place, and Amelia and Nathan by train to Indianapolis. Benjamin would remain for a time to see if Bill and Zeke made it to Terre Haute.

Annie had wanted to go with Jasper, but she had been dissuaded by threats to his safety. He promised to send for her when he could, but in the meantime, she would remain with the doctor and his wife.

Now that the time had come, Jenny couldn't bear the thought of leaving Benjamin. He had worked his way through her defenses, and she would never be the same again.

Probably she would remain an old maid for the rest of her

life. There was little chance that another man would find her as attractive as Benjamin seemed to. It still amazed her that she had somehow captured his attention. What was even more amazing was the fact that she would give up her freedom in a minute if it meant being with him.

Sighing, she pulled the quilt up closer to her chin and cuddled beneath its warm folds. It would be hard to leave Amelia, too. Knowing that she was safe with Nathan helped to lessen the pain, but not much. At least they would have a few more days together before they all parted, probably forever.

Still, it was not Amelia who filled her dreams that night but Benjamin. His strong arms reached out to her, promising her safety. Before she could respond, his vision disappeared.

❧

Jenny stood on the train platform, shivering against the cold November wind. Benjamin stood beside her, preoccupied with his own thoughts. Neither could find words, and so they remained silent, the minutes ticking slowly by.

Bustling up beside them, Mrs. Mitchell broke the silence.

"Here you are, dear. Something to eat on the train. Although they offer food, it's frightfully expensive."

She handed Jenny a sack, hugged her, and released her. "I'm going to miss you."

"I'll miss you, too, Mrs. Mitchell." Surprised, Jenny realized the truth of the statement. "I want to thank you so much for everything."

Jenny rubbed her hand down the blue wool dress that Mrs. Mitchell had given her, then patted the bun that the older woman had helped to arrange in her hair. For the first time in her life, Jenny felt like a real lady.

"You're more than welcome, dear." Glancing from Jenny to Benjamin, the doctor's wife stepped away from the platform to give them some privacy.

A muscle worked convulsively in Benjamin's jaw. His gaze drifted quickly over Jenny's body before finally reaching her eyes. Reluctantly, his hands moved over her shoulders like a butterfly afraid to settle. He was unused to this new Jenny, this sophisticated woman.

Jenny was not so reluctant. She placed her hands firmly on his chest, and leaning up, kissed him soundly on the lips.

He stiffened against her, but in the next instant he was pulling her closer, his arms wrapped securely around her. When their lips finally parted, Benjamin leaned his forehead against hers, his breathing heavy.

"Jenny."

She quickly placed her fingers against his lips. "Don't. There's nothing to say."

He pulled her hand away, his eyes on fire. "Except that I love you."

Sucking in a breath, Jenny smiled wryly. "*Now* you tell me."

The train's whistle pierced the cold morning air.

"All aboard!"

Benjamin frowned at the conductor's call. He needed more time. He should have talked to Jenny before, but he hadn't had an opportunity. His frustrated eyes met Jenny's.

"Jenny, do you love me?"

A few nights ago, she would have given him his answer in a second. Now, she hesitated. There was too much to talk over and not enough time to do it in.

"Jenny?"

He enclosed her face within the palms of his hands, forcing her to meet his look. Although her mouth hadn't yet uttered the words, he could read the truth in her eyes. He kissed her again, then took her by the arm and helped her to mount the steps to the passenger car.

"Wait for me, Jenny. Please. I'll be returning to Philadelphia soon. We'll talk then. My friends will meet you at the train and take care of you until I can return. Just wait for me."

Billows of steam rose around them as the train prepared to depart. A slight jerk, and the train began to move away. Benjamin followed, his steps increasing as the train gained momentum, his eyes never leaving Jenny's. He was at the edge of the platform before Jenny leaned over the railing and shouted.

"I'll wait."

❧

Jenny stared out the window at the drifting snow. In the panes she could see the reflection of the Barton's Christmas tree. In only five days it would be Christmas, and still Benjamin hadn't returned to Philadelphia.

The Bartons were the friends Benjamin had mentioned, and they were wonderful people. She was amazed that blacks could be so well off financially. Although the Barton house was certainly not on a scale with Mr. Jackson's plantation, it was much grander than anything Jenny had seen before. Benjamin was telling the truth when he said there were wealthy blacks in the North.

There was big news this day. South Carolina had seceded from the Union, and there was word that other states would probably follow. Jenny had no idea what that would mean for her, but she dreaded what it might mean for her family in Tennessee.

The Bartons had sent word to Mr. Jackson that she was alive and safe, and Jenny knew that he would inform her parents. As the date set aside for Christ's birth approached, she longed to see her family again.

Every year Mr. Jackson held a Christmas buffet for all the slaves on his plantation. Jenny's mouth almost watered thinking about the ham, turkey, apple walnut stuffing, and other wonderful foods. Mr. Jackson also gave each slave a gift of some sort. After listening to the others tell their stories of slavery, she was convinced that Mr. Jackson must be a special man. She regretted not noticing that before. Yet her parents knew.

Dropping the curtain back into place, Jenny turned back into the room, her hoop skirts bustling about her. The fine clothes had taken some getting used to. In Tennessee, only the finest ladies dressed so, but here in Philadelphia things were different. Although there were many blacks who were poor, there were also many who were not.

Her appearance was only one of the things that had changed about her. Jenny wanted so much to let Mama and Pappy know that she had finally surrendered her life to Christ. What a difference He had made in her attitude, in her very life. Her restlessness and uncertainty had flown in the face of the Master's love. She was learning to be content and to trust in God's guidance. It hadn't been an easy capitulation, but it was a complete one.

It occurred to her that Christ was what made the difference in people's lives. Christ made the Freemans risk their lives by sheltering darkies. Christ made Mr. Jackson the owner that he was. It was Christ who made Benjamin risk everything for people he didn't even know.

The lack of Christ also made Mr. Greer the abusive, cheating man that he was and Hawkins the cruel overseer that he was. Thankfully Amelia and Nathan were safe from them forever. Jenny had received word that her friends were secure and doing well in Canada.

Over a month had gone by, and still Benjamin had not come. He had sent word that he had been delayed, but that had been three weeks ago. Since that time they had received no further communication, and every day Jenny grew more fearful about his safety.

She wandered over to the tree, gently touching a glass ball that reflected the miniature candles clipped to the branches.

Lydia Barton breezed into the room, her hooped skirt swinging delicately about her. Her frizzy gray hair was tidied into a bun surrounded by a lace snood.

"Isn't it a lovely tree?"

Jenny nodded. "I always loved Christmas at home. That was when my whole family came together with all the other plantation slaves, and Mr. Jackson would read the Christmas story. I loved to hear the story of the little baby born in a manger."

More and more Jenny was picking up the correct manner of speech. She had meant it when she told Benjamin that her people spoke the way they did as a common bond, but here in the North things were so different. She didn't want Benjamin to be ashamed of her, and she didn't want others to think she was ignorant. Most people in the North accepted darkies as human beings, unlike the people in the South.

Lydia seated herself on the sofa. "Ah, but that was only a small part of what makes this such a special time. Not only was Jesus born, but He overcame death so that we might live."

They were interrupted by the arrival of Fenton Barton. He smiled at Jenny as he crossed the room to his wife. Leaning down, he gave her a brief kiss before turning to Jenny.

"I've heard from Benjamin."

Jenny felt her heart speed up to twice its rate. She waited for Fenton to continue.

"He should arrive in about three days."

"Did he. . .did he have a message for me?"

Husband and wife exchanged amused glances. Fenton seated himself beside his wife before answering.

"No, there was no more to the message than that he should arrive in about three days."

Disappointed, Jenny began to fiddle with her dress to hide her embarrassment. She had only recently been learning to trust in God's divine plan, and she wouldn't start to second-guess Him now. If Benjamin was coming to her, she would find out soon enough.

The maid announced that dinner was ready. That was another thing that Jenny was having a hard time coming to terms with. The maid was white, and she served a black family.

It was while they were eating their dessert, the maid came to announce that a police officer was at the door with another gentleman. Fenton directed her to show them into the parlor.

He was gone but a moment. When he returned, his dark features were unusually pale. The look he gave Jenny sent a thrill of fear winging its way through her middle.

"There's a man here that claims he has orders to return you to your master. He has a document to prove his ownership.

The magistrate has ordered your arrest, but I fear there is some mistake. This man claims that your name is Amelia."

Jenny dropped her fork, staring at Fenton aghast. She wasn't sure what she should do or even what she should think. It was as though her brain had suddenly stopped functioning. She rose slowly to her feet and one thought entered her head. *Run*!

Before she could act on the impulse, a police officer entered the dining room followed by Jeremiah Hawkins. The officer turned to the overseer.

"Is this the one?"

There was no mistaking the malevolent gleam in Hawkins's eyes. "Yeah. She's the one." He grinned at Jenny. "Time to go home, Amelia."

Lydia Barton moved forward. "You're mistaken. This girl's name is Jenny, not Amelia."

The officer nodded his head in Hawkins's direction. "This man has a document claiming otherwise. The magistrate has ordered that she be turned over to him in accordance with the Fugitive Slave Act of 1850."

"But he's lying," Jenny shouted.

Fenton Barton placed himself in Hawkins's way. "I demand a trial," he growled, his eyes promising retribution.

Hawkins was unmoved. "I don't know how people deal with darkies up here in the North, but I'd suggest you git outta my way."

The officer was apologetic. "I'm sorry, but it's the law."

No one noticed the Barton maid hurry out the front door. Jenny and Hawkins were locked in a feud of eyes, neither relenting. The challenge in Hawkins's eyes was met and matched by the defiance in Jenny's.

"Now you don't want these good people to git hurt, do you?" Hawkins asked softly as he pushed back his jacket to reveal his pistol.

The police officer intervened, his voice vibrant with anger. "Now look here. We don't threaten people in their own homes here."

Hawkins's eyes never wavered from Jenny's. She got the message.

"I'll go."

"No, Jenny." Fenton Barton turned his wrath on Hawkins. "Get out of my house!"

"I'm going. *With* my slave."

Jenny placed a restraining hand on Fenton's arm. "Please, Mr. Barton. I don't want anything to happen to Lydia."

Jerking his eyes to his wife, Jenny could see his shoulders deflate. Jenny went past him and halted in front of Hawkins.

"I'll go with you, Mr. Hawkins, but God will deal with you."

His lips curled into a sneer, and snickering, he told her, "I'll take my chances."

Taking Jenny's arm in a brutal grip, he jerked her toward the door. Jenny looked over her shoulder, tears held firmly in check. "Tell Benjamin that I waited."

Lydia dissolved into a puddle of tears while her husband clenched and unclenched his jaw. "I'll tell him. Don't worry, Jenny. We'll find you."

Hawkins yanked her down the front steps, the cold wind whipping about them as he pushed her into a wagon. He crawled up beside her and, snapping his whip, he sent the horses skidding through the gathering snow. Since Hawkins hadn't given her any opportunity to gather a wrap to protect herself, Jenny wrapped her arms around herself, trying to stave off the bitter cold. Seemingly oblivious to the cold himself, Hawkins only grinned at Jenny's discomfort. His words froze Jenny's insides as thoroughly as the wind chilled her outside.

"Let's see how high and mighty Jackson feels now! Call me a bulldog, will he?" He threw back his head and cackled. "Well, I guess maybe I am. But I guess this old bulldog's gonna have the last laugh."

They were no more than two streets away when they were stopped by several men standing in the street. Surprised, Hawkins pulled back on the reins. "Whoa!" He glared at the men. "Are you crazy! Get outta the road!"

Before he could say any more, the wagon was surrounded by a mob. Jenny understood before Hawkins did, and taking advantage of the opportunity, she jumped from the wagon.

Hawkins lunged for her, but he was met by a fist in the face that sent him flipping to the icy ground. Never having been confronted by such an angry mob before, he was wise enough to stay put when several men came and stood over him.

"Get out of our city, you flea-ridden vermin!"

Hawkins had heard of vigilante mobs, but he hadn't really believed they existed. It boggled his mind that so many white folks would band together to protect darkies. As his eyes slid slowly over the group, he realized that almost half of them were black.

"Go back to your own evil state," another told him.

Slowly Hawkins got to his feet. Only now did he realize that Jackson's slave was missing. Mouth set in a grim line, he faced the crowd challengingly.

"That slave belongs to me."

An egg landed on the side of his head, soon followed by another, then another. Heart pounding in fear, Hawkins climbed in his wagon and charged the horses through the crowd of people, their taunts and jeers sounding in his ears long after he had disappeared from their sight.

thirteen

"Gone! What do you mean she's gone?" Benjamin stared at his friend in stunned amazement. Jenny gone! How was that possible? He had been so certain that she would wait for him. Perhaps it had been unwise to stay away so long, but things had happened in Terre Haute to necessitate his remaining.

Fenton explained everything that had transpired only two nights before. When he finished, he told Benjamin rather lamely, "She told me to tell you that she waited."

Benjamin blew out a slow breath, collapsing to the sofa behind him.

"Our maid, Myra, went to the Philadelphia Female Anti-Slavery Society for help." Mrs. Barton smiled at her maid. "We didn't even know she was a member."

Myra addressed herself to Benjamin. "We didn't think it would be wise to bring Jenny back here. That Mr. Hawkins didn't seem like the type to give up too easily."

Benjamin stared off into the distance as he tried to remember all the things Jenny had told him about the overseer. He had no idea why the man would claim Jenny was Amelia unless he planned to sell Jenny without anyone's knowledge.

"No," he told them remotely, his thoughts still with Jenny. "He probably wouldn't."

"Anyway," Myra continued, "we took her to others who would protect her."

"I need to see her."

Fenton slapped him on the back, his hearty voice ringing throughout the room. "We know, Benjamin. But it's not safe just yet. Although the mob managed to run Mr. Hawkins off, he's still in Philadelphia."

The gleam in Benjamin's eye didn't bode well for the

overseer should they happen to cross paths.

Lydia patted his arm in understanding. "Patience, Benjamin. Remember, patience is a virtue."

Not so long ago Benjamin had believed himself to have plenty of that particular virtue. Now he found that he had been fooling himself. His patience was fast running out. He wanted Jenny to be with him so that he could care for her. Protect her. Having taken so long to come to her, would she believe that of him now?

Bill and Zeke had been brought to Terre Haute shortly after the others had departed, but it had taken him some time to locate Lila and Harriet and finally get them together. He felt good about that, but it stretched the time considerably when he had wanted to come to Philadelphia. Still, he wouldn't give up on a job once he had been committed. Personal happiness had to wait. Benjamin believed that in the end, God would reward him for his faithfulness.

"Come and let us have supper," Fenton advised.

Food was the last thing on Benjamin's mind. When he set himself a course of action, he was like a mule until he accomplished that purpose. This time, however, he knew he would have to restrain his impulses. It bothered him extremely that he had been brought to this point in his life when he had least expected it.

Smiling crookedly, he followed the Bartons into the dining room. God's ways were not his ways, and he felt it best not to try and second-guess his Lord. Anytime he tried, he wound up in big trouble.

❧

Benjamin walked through the streets of Philadelphia on Christmas Eve oblivious to the cold, the snow, or even the cheer. Carolers wandered the streets, stopping periodically to sing to the bustling crowd of people. The scene reminded him of the Charles Dickens book, *A Christmas Carol*. The Scrooge in this whole scenario was Jeremiah Hawkins, but unlike that fictional character, Benjamin doubted that a visit from three spirits would change the hard-bitten overseer.

Benjamin was on his way to see Jenny, and Hawkins or no, he was going to ask her to marry him. Lydia had told him about Jenny's surrender to Jesus Christ. He knew without a doubt that it hadn't happened overnight. For Jenny it must have been quite a struggle, but how would that affect her relationship to him? He rather enjoyed the fiery, willful woman she was.

Remembering the story Myra had told him of Jenny's getaway, he grinned. No, he doubted that stubborn spirit was gone, and if she accepted his proposal, he knew his life would never be boring.

Tomorrow was Christmas, and hidden in his pocket was Jenny's Christmas present. The amber nugget ring reminded him of her eyes in the sunshine. The modest diamonds that surrounded it gave an added sparkle to the stone that also reminded him of Jenny's eyes, especially when they were full of tears or sparkling with anger.

He hurried his steps, eager to get an answer from the one woman whom he knew would make his life complete. So intense were his thoughts that he was unaware of the figure skulking along in his wake.

❧

Jenny watched Benjamin come from her vantage point at the top of the brownstone mansion. Her heart was thundering in panic, and she was suddenly uncertain of the reception she might receive. She pulled herself from the window of the upper story bedroom and began to pace. Any moment now he would knock at the door and ask for her, and then what? What should she say? What *could* she say?

The maid knocked on the door to announce her visitor. As she followed the girl downstairs, her frightened heart was lifted in prayer. If only God would give her some indication that what she intended was truly the right thing to do. Closing her eyes briefly, she remembered the last time that she and Benjamin were together. That kiss on the railroad platform now seemed so far away and so long ago. Perhaps he had changed his mind about her.

He hadn't. Jenny knew it as soon as she looked into his mahogany brown eyes. The look of love almost smothered her with its intensity. Unbeknownst to her, her own eyes were answering in kind.

After the maid closed the door behind her, they were alone. For a long moment neither one knew what to say. Benjamin finally broke the silence.

"You look beautiful."

Heat flooded into her cheeks, and she glanced away in embarrassment. "It's the clothes."

His warm eyes never left her face. "The clothes are nice, but that's not what makes you beautiful."

She snorted lightly. "I've never been beautiful, Benjamin. The clothes help me look proper, but I'll never be beautiful."

Taking her hands in his, he lifted them to his lips, kissing them softly. "Must you always argue?"

He saw the flames leap into her eyes, and he grinned. *There* was his Jenny.

Jenny saw the humor lurking in his eyes and her protest died in her throat. It never occurred to her to be shy or reticent. That was not her way. She wrapped her arms around his neck and, closing her eyes, invited his kiss.

He didn't disappoint her. It was sometime later before either one was ready for conversation.

Benjamin held her close in his arms, his cheek resting on her head. "I'm sorry I wasn't here when you needed me," he told her huskily.

"You're here now," she responded. "And God was there all the time. If you had been there, I wouldn't have relied on Him, and He knew I needed the practice."

Smiling, Benjamin pulled away slightly so that he could see her face. As they studied the messages in each other's eyes, all doubts soon fled. They found they needed no other words.

"Will you marry me, Jenny?"

The smile slowly slipped from Benjamin's face as a shutter

seemed to come down over Jenny's features. She pulled out of his arms and moved away. The sudden chill in the room had nothing to do with the decreasing temperatures outside.

"I can't, Benjamin," she answered him gently.

Mystified, he followed her to the sofa and seated himself next to her. Only his iron will kept him from pulling her into his arms and demanding an explanation. His patience was rewarded when she finally turned to him and with tears in her eyes told him, "I have to go back to Tennessee."

His mouth dropped open. "What? Who says?"

"God."

Benjamin's mind reeled at the implication. Who had told her such a thing?

"Benjamin," she continued, "have you read the Book of Philemon in the Bible?"

His mind rapidly switching gears, Benjamin tried to remember what the Book of Philemon said. He usually kept his studies to the four Gospels.

"Refresh my memory."

"A slave named Onesimus ran away from his master. He eventually found the Apostle Paul and spent time with him. After coming to believe in Jesus, Paul sent Onesimus back to his master after pleading for his life and safety. I feel I have to go back."

Rubbing a hand across his forehead, Benjamin frowned. "That was almost two thousand years ago."

It was a lame argument, and he knew it. Jenny reminded him, "You once told me that Jesus Christ is the same yesterday, today, and forever."

His blazing eyes met hers. "Yes, but Paul also admonished Philemon to do what was right. Since he was an elder in the church, he could have *ordered* Philemon to, but he asked him as a brother. It's *wrong* to own slaves."

"But he still sent Onesimus back."

Aggravated, Benjamin got to his feet. He was so frustrated, he didn't know which way to turn. He knew that once Jenny set her mind to something, there would be no swaying her.

"I have to go back, Benjamin. It's the only way to make things right, and I want to start my new life in Christ without any blemishes."

Kneeling beside the sofa, Benjamin gripped her shoulders. "Honey, you need to think about this some more."

She dropped her eyes to her lap. "It's all I've thought about for days. My mind's made up."

Shoving his hands into his pockets, he struggled to keep from shaking some sense into her. His hand found the ring box and closed tightly around it. Could he persuade her to change her mind? Somehow, he doubted it.

A knock on the door interrupted them. The maid peeked her head in the room.

"There's a gentleman here to see you, Miss Jenny."

An odd sense of déjà vu beset Jenny. A strange foreboding settled around her like a shroud. She was on her feet in an instant.

"Wait!"

The maid had already disappeared from sight, returning a moment later with Jeremiah Hawkins and the same police officer from several days ago. Unconsciously, Jenny moved to Benjamin's side for protection. The overseer laughed without mirth, and Jenny felt a sudden thrill of fear.

Benjamin's eyes were like brown chips of ice. "Let me guess. You must be Hawkins."

Hawkins looked for a place to spit, realized his whereabouts, and shifted the wad of tobacco in his mouth.

"And you must be the darkie that's been hijacking slave coffles," Hawkins answered, tobacco juice running down his chin. Wiping his mouth on his sleeve, he looked from Benjamin to Jenny. "And it looks like you're trying to hijack my slave now."

Benjamin's very stillness should have been a warning, but it went unheeded. When Hawkins came closer to Jenny, he found himself instead confronted by a formfitting waistcoat. The size of Benjamin was enough to intimidate even the overseer.

"You'll not touch her."

Although the words were spoken softly, there was no denying their effect. Hawkins took a quick step back as the police officer came forward. The officer's eyes met Benjamin's across the overseer's head, and they flickered with recognition.

"He has a legal document. The magistrate ordered that the woman be turned over to him."

"Let me see the document."

Reluctantly, Hawkins handed the paper into Benjamin's outstretched hand. Benjamin's gaze went swiftly over the form before coming back to the police officer.

"This paper says it's for a slave named Amelia. This woman's name is Jenny."

"So she says," Hawkins grated. "I should know my own slave." His eyes began to gleam as he studied Benjamin. "Come to think of it, you resemble the description of a runaway from a plantation close to ours."

"No!" Horrified, Jenny turned her attention to the police officer. "He's not a slave! He's from Philadelphia."

The officer nodded. "I know that, ma'am. Dr. Walters is well known here in Philadelphia."

Hawkins's jaw dropped and it took him a moment to recover his poise. Angrily, he told the officer, "Well, that ain't got nothing to do with this here woman. She's my slave, and I'm taking her with me."

It was hard to make good on the threat when Benjamin stood unyieldingly between them.

"As I said. You're not taking her anywhere."

"I agree."

The voice that spoke came from the open doorway. Hawkins whirled to face Adam Jackson standing on the threshold. The plantation owner looked like a vengeful warrior about to do battle.

"Jackson!"

The older man entered the room, handing his gloves and

jacket to the maid. He glanced at Jenny, his eyes going wide at her unaccustomed apparel. A slow smile spread across his face, but didn't quite make it to his eyes.

"I knew as soon as they told me at the telegraph office that you had read my telegraph from the Bartons that you would hightail it up here," he told Hawkins. He turned his attention to Jenny. "The Bartons told me where to find you. Your father and mother have been worried sick."

Jenny thought she must be dreaming. She tried several times to speak, but couldn't get her mouth to cooperate. She felt betrayed by the Bartons, yet knew there must be a reason they would send Mr. Jackson here.

Adam Jackson confronted the officer. "This slave is mine, not Mr. Hawkins's. Mr. Hawkins doesn't even own a slave. He merely works for a plantation owner in Tennessee."

The officer's look went from Adam back to Benjamin. At Benjamin's confirming nod, he turned an angry countenance on Hawkins.

"I trust Dr. Walters's word. If you wish to dispute this matter, you might like to have the magistrate review your complaint."

The color drained from Hawkins's face. He glared in impotent fury at each man, his look finally resting on Adam. Without saying a word, he spun on his heels and slammed out of the room. The officer nodded at everyone and hastily followed.

Adam spared a look for Benjamin before he concentrated his attention on Jenny. Before he could say anything, Benjamin stepped forward.

"I think you should know that I won't allow you to take Jenny."

Instead of being angry, Adam's face registered amusement. "I see." His examination once again settled on Jenny's uncertain face. She met his eyes unwaveringly.

"I was going to come back," she told him softly.

"Were you?" His gaze moved to the sofa. "May we sit down?"

Jenny nodded. The owners of the house had gone to New York for the holidays and had given her free rein of the household. They were a kind white couple who had never had any children of their own, and they had taken Jenny under their wing. They had even offered to take her with them to New York, but she had declined, knowing that Benjamin was due to arrive any day.

"I found Jesus, Master Jackson," Jenny told him. "That's why I was going to come back."

Adam didn't answer right away. Instead he asked Benjamin sternly, "And you are?"

Without hesitation, Benjamin answered him. "I'm the man who's going to marry Jenny."

Jenny sucked in her breath at the audacity of the statement. She couldn't bring herself to look at either man.

"Indeed. And when is the happy day?"

Jenny spoke before Benjamin could answer. "There isn't going to be any happy day. I told you, Master Jackson, I was coming home." Her eyelashes dropped to veil her eyes.

Only by clenching his teeth tightly together could Benjamin keep from shouting that Adam Jackson was not her master. His own fierce look more than matched that of the plantation owner.

"Tell me about this man, Jenny."

Jenny told how she and Benjamin had met and about their travels together. There was a wealth of respect in the look Adam bestowed upon the young black man.

"And do you love him?"

Jenny didn't even think to deny it. She nodded her head, her warm brown eyes entwining with Benjamin's.

"Then I'll sell her to you."

Never had Adam been so alarmed as when faced with such a wrathful giant. As Benjamin came up off the sofa, his fists were clenched at his sides. Adam reared backward against the sofa holding his palms up. For a moment, he genuinely feared for his life.

"Hear me out, young man."

Jenny had always wondered if Benjamin had a temper. Having never seen it before, she was a little amazed by his fury now.

"Jenny has already admitted that she was going to return home. That she is a sister in Christ is a blessing to me and I know will be to her parents. I have no doubt that you are responsible for this in a significant way. Still, I respect Jenny's decision, and I can even understand it in a way." He smiled at Jenny. "In my state, it is illegal to free your slaves, but I *can* sell them."

"I don't have that kind of money."

Jenny's head snapped up at the intensity of Benjamin's voice.

Surprised, Adam shrugged and lifted his hands outward. "I don't understand. I hadn't intended to ask much."

"There isn't enough money in the world that could satisfy that debt. Jenny is priceless."

Sudden understanding filled Adam's features. He smiled at Jenny, who had dropped her eyes at the fervent announcement.

"I agree. Still, the law is the law. Would you consider five dollars a worthy investment?"

Benjamin pulled his wallet from his jacket and quickly withdrew the required amount. Before he handed Adam the money, his questioning eyes met Jenny's.

"Is this acceptable to you?"

Smiling, she nodded. Didn't he know that she already belonged to him? Her heart and her mind would forever be his.

Benjamin handed Adam the money, and Adam reached into his own jacket to retrieve Jenny's slave papers. He relinquished them to Benjamin, a wry smile twisting his lips.

"It's not against the law to free slaves in the North."

"No," Benjamin told him diffidently. "But I'm breaking the law by *buying* one." He handed Jenny her slave papers. "You better burn these before we *all* get into trouble."

"With pleasure," she told him happily. Going to the fireplace, she quickly tossed the papers in. They watched as the document was quickly eaten up by the flames.

When Adam spoke again, he was much more serious.

"Jenny, I'm going to sell all the slaves on my plantation."

She turned quickly from the fire, her eyes going wide.

"I have arranged to have several abolitionists make the purchase, and then they will in turn set them free. Those who want to remain with me can do so. It's the only thing I could think of to do." There was pain in his voice when he continued. "I've also arranged to sell my plantation. I'll be moving my family north. I'm afraid that with South Carolina seceding from the Union, others will follow. I've heard the talk even in Tennessee. There's no doubt in my mind that we are going to be faced with some terrible consequences."

"Mama and Pappy?"

"We talked about it, and they want to go to Indiana."

"But why? Why can't they come here?"

"Jes wants to homestead, and your parents want to see their first grandchild. Can you blame them?"

No, she couldn't. After all, it hadn't been Jes that ran away and left them. Besides, her parents would be much more comfortable in Indiana, where there was more space and land than here in this city among the crowds of people.

Adam walked over and took Jenny by the shoulders. "I'll tell them your good news. They will be so happy for both your marriage and your salvation."

"I appreciate that. I'm so sorry that it took me so long to realize what a good man you are. Thank you, Master Jackson."

He shook her lightly. "I'm not your master anymore."

The thought would take some getting used to. Even when she was running for freedom, she had never felt really unfettered.

Smiling, Adam released her. Turning to Benjamin, he offered his hand. "Take good care of her."

"I intend to."

They surveyed each other briefly, both liking what they saw. As the door shut behind Adam, Jenny felt a sudden sense of loss. She crossed to the window, watching as Adam Jackson climbed into his carriage and quickly departed. Searching the dark winter sky, she found her northern compass. She had come so far in such a short period of time. It was almost as though she was another person from that ragged, ignorant woman of the past. She had drunk from the sky, from that bright gourd of freedom, and she would never be the same again.

She felt Benjamin's hands settle warmly on her shoulders. He turned her to face him.

"*Now* will you marry me?"

It was hard to speak past the lump in her throat. She tried several times before she could finally get the words out.

"Oh, Benjamin. God has been so good!"

Folding her into his arms, he told her softly, "Oh, Jenny. The best is yet to be."

A Letter To Our Readers

Dear Reader:

In order that we might better contribute to your reading enjoyment, we would appreciate your taking a few minutes to respond to the following questions. We welcome your comments and read each form and letter we receive. When completed, please return to the following:

Rebecca Germany, Fiction Editor
Heartsong Presents
PO Box 719
Uhrichsville, Ohio 44683

1. Did you enjoy reading *Drink from the Sky?*

   ❑ Very much. I would like to see more books by this author!

   ❑ Moderately

   I would have enjoyed it more if ____________________

   ____

   ____

2. Are you a member of **Heartsong Presents**? Yes ❑ No ❑

   If no, where did you purchase this book?____________

   ____

3. How would you rate, on a scale from 1 (poor) to 5 (superior), the cover design?____________________

4. On a scale from 1 (poor) to 10 (superior), please rate the following elements.

   _____ Heroine _____ Plot

   _____ Hero _____ Inspirational theme

   _____ Setting _____ Secondary characters

5. These characters were special because________________

____

____

6. How has this book inspired your life?________________

____

____

7. What settings would you like to see covered in future **Heartsong Presents** books?________________

____

____

8. What are some inspirational themes you would like to see treated in future books?________________

____

____

9. Would you be interested in reading other **Heartsong Presents** titles? Yes ❑ No ❑

10. Please check your age range:

❑ Under 18 ❑ 18-24 ❑ 25-34

❑ 35-45 ❑ 46-55 ❑ Over 55

11. How many hours per week do you read?________________

Name ______________________________________

Occupation __________________________________

Address ____________________________________

City ________________ State ____________ Zip ____________